RILKA DRAGNEVA AND
KATARYNA WOLCZUK

SOVEREIGNTY, PATRIMONY AND INTERNATIONAL LAW

Russia's Attack on Ukraine

BRISTOL
UNIVERSITY
PRESS

First published in Great Britain in 2026 by

Bristol University Press
University of Bristol
1–9 Old Park Hill
Bristol
BS2 8BB
UK
t: +44 (0)117 374 6645
e: bup-info@bristol.ac.uk

Details of international sales and distribution partners are available at bristoluniversitypress.co.uk

DOI: 10.51952/9781529242812

British Library Cataloguing in Publication Data
A catalogue record for this book is available from the British Library

ISBN 978-1-5292-4279-9 hardcover
ISBN 978-1-5292-4280-5 ePub
ISBN 978-1-5292-4281-2 ePdf

Cover design: blu inc
Front cover image: GettyImages/Liyao Xie

To my sister, Petya Dragneva,
with love and gratitude
RD

To my parents,
Annelia and Wlodzimierz
KW

Contents

ONE

Framing Russia's Attack on Ukraine's Statehood

In February 2022, Russia launched a full-scale military invasion of Ukraine, despite having repeatedly affirmed its recognition of Ukrainian sovereignty. Since 1991 Moscow had consistently pledged to respect Ukraine's sovereignty in accordance with international law. The invasion precipitated a brutal and costly war whose repercussions extend far beyond Europe, shaking – indeed undermining – the very foundations of the post-1945 international order.

Numerous explanations have been put forward to explain the causes of the war. Yet none offer a fully satisfactory explanation for the seismic shift from Russia's unequivocal recognition of Ukraine's statehood to the denial of its very right to exist. The empirical and analytical challenge is compounded by the narratives emanating from Moscow: ranging from initial denials of Russia's aggression, to ethno-historical justifications, to a catalogue of grievances directed at the West – and seemingly everything in between. Even as missiles pummelled Ukrainian cities and Russian tanks rolled toward Kyiv, President Putin maintained: 'We have been treating all new post-Soviet states with respect and will continue to act this way. We respect and will respect their sovereignty.'[1]

1 Address by the President of the Russian Federation, 24 February 2022, http://en.kremlin.ru/events/president/news/67843.

This book aims to clarify this complex and often misunderstood picture. It contends that Russia's invasion should not be interpreted as a volte face, but rather a continuation of its long-standing objectives toward Ukraine through different means. Drawing on extensive and compelling evidence, we argue that since 1991 Russia's approach to Ukraine has been shaped by a patrimonial paradigm, one that has consistently informed its policy decisions. Accordingly, Russia's attack on Ukraine was not an ad hoc act but the escalation of a broader strategy rooted in a tradition of instrumentalizing sovereignty and (international) law. In other words, Russia did not simply cease to be a 'good citizen' and violate international law. Rather, the invasion represented the logical progression following the failure of its preferred model for asserting patrimonial claims over Ukraine in the post-Soviet period. This book is about the anatomy of this failure.

The cloak of 'normality'

At the heart of the difficulty in explaining Russia's conduct in 2022 lies a widely held assumption that in 1991, albeit reluctantly, Russia accepted Ukraine's statehood. Following the dissolution of the Soviet Union, Russia formally recognized Ukraine's independence and committed to conducting interstate relations in accordance with international law. Over the subsequent two decades, Moscow signed a plethora of bilateral and regional agreements affirming its respect for Ukraine's sovereignty and territorial integrity. These commitments were further reinforced by Russia's international obligations as a Union of the Soviet Socialist Republics (USSR) continuation state in the United Nations (UN), assuming its Security Council seat but also resubscribing to the norms of the UN Charter and the Helsinki Final Act, both of which explicitly prohibit the revision of borders by force.

Moscow appeared particularly eager to signal a break with its imperial and Communist past. This was despite the fact that, until that point, Russia had never dealt with the post-Soviet states outside a polity it controlled. President Yeltsin declared that Russia would be an 'honest and reliable partner' with which the formerly subservient republics could 'cooperate on the basis of the generally accepted norms of international law',[2] a stance unprecedented in Russian history. Yet old habits proved difficult to abandon. Moscow began referring to the former Soviet republics as its 'near abroad' and 'post-Soviet space' (*prostranstvo*), thereby creating a conceptual grey zone: external, but not entirely foreign. This semantic framing enabled Russia to assert special rights within this ambiguous space, including the responsibility for 'maintenance of peace and the protection of compatriots abroad', while presenting such claims as 'the normal vision of geopolitical interests' of a normal great power.[3] As Foreign Minister Andrei Kozyrev put it, Russia was to assume a 'special but not imperial' role, while acting 'as an integral part of the global system of international relations that is subordinate to universal norms'.[4]

In the early 1990s, the West was highly receptive to the vision of new, 'normalized' Russia. As anxieties over potential chaos and instability, once feared to erupt from the 'Soviet cauldron' (Office of Soviet Analysis, 1991), began to subside, the peaceful dissolution of the former superpower and the resolution of the Soviet nuclear arsenal issue fostered a sense of euphoria. Liberal democracy appeared to have triumphed, and a peace dividend was anticipated. In the bigger scheme of things, how Russia – despite its proclamations – was actually behaving toward its neighbours, was of marginal interest. After all, the membership in the international order, championed

---

2 'Boris Yeltsin addresses Minsk Summit', Television First Channel, 16 April 1993 (in Brzezinski and Sullivan, 1997: 82).

3 'Andrey Kozirev outlines foreign policy priorities', *Nezavisimaya Gazeta*, 20 August 1992 (in Brzezinski and Sullivan, 1997: 78).

4 'Andrey Kozirev on Russia's peacekeeping role in the CIS', *Nezavisimaya Gazeta*, 22 September 1993 (in Brzezinski and Sullivan, 1997: 82).

by both Gorbachev and Yeltsin, implied that Russia would adopt not only its laws, but perhaps more importantly, the norms and values underpinning them. It seemed that the globalization of the international order had simply extended eastward (Ikenberry, 2018).

Moscow's claims over and policies toward the post-Soviet 'space' were acknowledged. The West did not formally grant Russia rights or privileges in response to its demands for a special regional status, yet it effectively acquiesced to Moscow's assertion of a 'sphere of interest'. An unspoken understanding emerged: as long as Russia did not rock the systemic boat, its claims and self-appointed role would go largely unquestioned and unopposed. The narrative that Russia was a post-imperial rather than a neo-imperial state (Trenin, 2011) proved sufficient for Western officials, experts and scholars, who accepted the associated request for time and space to grieve and normalize. The protracted and complex process of 'establishing friendly relations' between Ukraine and Russia, including the affirmation of statehood and inviolability of borders, was interpreted as part of the 'normalization' of Russia, as it slowly came to terms with the new post-Soviet realities (D'Anieri, 2012).

This 'normalization' agenda led academics and policy makers to shift their focus elsewhere. As local disputes over undefined borders, long-standing historical grievances, and frozen conflicts proliferated across obscure corners of the post-Soviet region, fatigue with the area began to set in. Consequently, the region became the domain of an increasingly narrow group of specialists. Among them, few possessed the linguistic skills, let alone the interest, necessary to engage with the legal intricacies of bilateral relations. Expertise became increasingly bifurcated: while most scholars concentrated on Russia's relations with the West, relatively little attention was paid to its policies toward the Eastern European countries. Russia's self-ascribed privileged position in the region was, in effect, tacitly accepted.

In the absence of close scrutiny, and with the atrophy of historical anchoring, the continuity in Russia's approaches was glossed over. Any transgressions involving Russia were downplayed, or blamed on the disrespect for Russian sensitivities demonstrated by the West or the neighbouring states (Tsygankov, 2010; Menon and Rumer, 2015; Lieven, 2022). Interestingly, even sceptics of Russia's intentions toward its neighbours concluded that 'despite Moscow's wishes, each of the states is more or less able to defend its sovereignty and independence, thus limiting Russia's sway over the territory of the post-Soviet space' (Saivetz, 2012: 401). Thus, the prevailing view held that, given the inherited interdependencies, Russia's influence was understandable, yet Moscow was uninterested in or, at least incapable of, restoring the empire (Dawisha, 1997). If anything, many in the West simply welcomed Moscow's self-proclaimed role in the region, believing Russia would evolve into the benevolent and responsible hegemon it claimed to be, one that would oversee peace and spearhead the modernization of the post-Soviet 'space' (Wolczuk, 2021).

From 'normality' to aggression

The full-scale invasion of Ukraine in 2022 shattered illusions. In response, two broad explanations have emerged to account for Russia's apparent deviation from the presumed 'normality'. The first attributes the invasion to external provocation; the second views it as the outcome of a neo-imperial turn within Putin's Russia, driven by domestic dynamics.

Proponents of the first perspective, primarily international relations scholars and historians of Russia, argue that Russia was simply defending itself from the West's encroachment, manifested in NATO enlargement, European Union (EU) expansion and democracy promotion. They advocate a realist 'proxy war' thesis, positing that Russia's actions constitute a legitimate response to the provocation of others (Mearsheimer,

2014, 2022; Lieven, 2022; Walt, 2022). The logic of power-based international relations dictates that, like any great power, Russia needs a security perimeter or a sphere of influence to thwart other great powers. Some variations on the realist spectrum notwithstanding (Edinger, 2022), the overarching paradigm relies on system-level explanations that focus on interactions among a limited group of states. Within this paradigm, empirical evidence – beyond the assertion of threat, security concerns or provocation – is often considered unnecessary.

The criticisms of realism and its application to the Russia and Ukraine context are extensive and cannot be fully addressed here (see, for example, Motyl, 2015; Mälksoo, 2022; Dutkiewicz and Smolenski, 2023; Götz and Ekman, 2024; Hendl et al, 2024). However, two key arguments stand out. First, realist interpretations centre on great power rivalry, thereby sidelining domestic factors in both Russia and Ukraine, such as public opinion, economic conditions and, crucially, historical, cultural and ideational factors that both connect and divide the two countries. Such an approach also conveniently disregards the deeply historical nature of the war. Thus, the realists are not interested in, and offer no explanation for, the Russian leadership's denial of Ukraine's right to exist, nor for Russia's persistent inability to reconcile itself with Ukraine's statehood. Instead, the role of the West in general and NATO in particular is vastly exaggerated.

Second, the realist theory oversimplifies the complex and multifaceted interactions that have shaped Russia–Ukraine relations not only over the past three decades, but over the last three centuries. This reflects a pragmatic preference for stylized, parsimonious explanations that sacrifice conceptual and empirical depth for elegance. By treating Kyiv as a passive pawn in a 'sphere of influence' or a 'buffer zone', this framing fails to account for the evolving dynamics of Russia–Ukraine relations over time and, more importantly, for the extent to which Ukraine has claimed and will continue to claim agency, much to the chagrin of both Moscow and Western proponents of realism.

Another influential perspective interprets Russia's attack on Ukraine's statehood as an attempt at neo-imperial revival, underpinned by civilizational identity narratives. The shift is often attributed to Vladimir Putin, whose self-ascribed 'mission' is to restore Russia's historical imperial greatness and reincorporate lands deemed part of its 'state-civilization' (Linde, 2016; Hill and Stent, 2022; Götz and Ekman, 2024). This sense of mission became particularly pronounced with the onset of Putin's third presidential term in 2012, coinciding with a broader embrace of political and cultural conservatism (Laruelle, 2013; Makarychev and Yatsyk, 2014; Polyakov, 2015; Lewis, 2020) and authoritarianism (Popova and Shevel, 2023). The foreign policy implications of these domestic developments were most clearly expressed in the Kremlin's ambition to return Ukraine to its 'rightful' historical place within the Russian world.

This perspective offers powerful and valuable insights into the imperial undertones of Russia's actions and its objectives in Ukraine, highlighting Russia's self-assumed authority to 'tell others who they are and what choices are open to them' (Sherr and Gretskiy, 2023: 6). It aptly recognizes the role of historical legacies. Nevertheless, these debates often tend to presume Russia's acceptance of Ukraine's sovereignty in 1991, and thus focus on identifying the moment or trigger when Russia 'snapped'. What remains underexplored is the trajectory leading up to this neo-imperial turn, including its twists and adaptations. Given the fragmented picture, it is also difficult to explain why this revival culminated in full-scale invasion in 2022 and not earlier (Götz and Ekman, 2024).

This book addresses the limitations of these two broad explanations by foregrounding Russia's long-standing sense of historical entitlement to Ukraine. We emphasize the extent to which the contemporary Russian state has been shaped by legacies inherited from both the Soviet and tsarist pasts, and 'bears the imprint of doctrines, disciplines and habits acquired over a considerable period of time in relations with subjects, clients and independent states' (Sherr, 2013: 17–18). We demonstrate how Russia's sense of entitlement survived and was enacted across different phases, often under varying legal guises, including the grudging, instrumental acceptance of Ukrainian statehood in 1991. We argue that this was not a genuine acceptance, but rather a temporary concession: a stopgap on the path to eventual reunification. Ukraine's loyalty was presumed, and its return expected to be a matter of time.

However, integrating Ukraine into a new union proved far more challenging than anticipated in Moscow. Russia deployed a plethora of legal and extra-legal tools to nudge Ukraine toward reintegration with Russia, but to no avail. Thus, the book emphasizes the significant degree of agency exercised by Ukraine in resisting reabsorption and asserting its sovereignty. Faced with Ukraine's persistent defiance, Moscow shifted from diplomatic pressure to covert coercion in 2014, culminating in open warfare in 2022. In tracing this trajectory, we offer a nuanced analysis of why Russia felt compelled to launch a full-scale invasion of Ukraine and deny Ukraine's very existence as a state and nation.

Addressing the puzzle

Central to our explanation is an analysis of Russia's distinctive approach to power, sovereignty and international law, and the fundamental continuities within this approach. To advance this analysis, we develop a novel interdisciplinary framework that integrates insights from history, law and area studies. Our argument unfolds through three interconnected strands.

Russia's entitlement over Ukraine

Our starting point is the observation that Russia's understanding of sovereignty is fundamentally bifurcated: it distinguishes sharply between its own sovereignty and that of other states. This is not a formal distinction made by modern Russian law. Formally, in 1989 Moscow abandoned the doctrine of limited sovereignty that had characterized Soviet relations with its Central and Eastern European satellites during the Cold War. It declared a move to universalist notions of sovereignty and sovereign equality, granting an unprecedented supremacy of international law within its domestic legal hierarchy (Danilenko, 1999). Indeed, Russian legal scholarship asserts that state sovereignty is absolute, indivisible and cannot be limited in legal terms (Moiseev, 2009).

However, since the early 2000s, this universalist stance has undergone significant qualifications (Mälksoo, 2015; Kaczmarska, 2015; Bettiza and Lewis, 2020). Legal commentary and political statements increasingly reflected Moscow's growing discomfort with the liberal undertones of international law, particularly its emphasis on democracy, human rights and global governance. Russia began to position itself as a defender of traditional sovereignty, non-intervention and normative neutrality at the international level, a stance consistent with a pluralist vision of the international society (Allison, 2012).[5] Yet, far less attention has been paid to the extent to which Russia's actions in Eastern Europe since 1991 have aligned with – or deviated from – these professed principles of traditional sovereignty.

As Allison (2012) observed, in its self-proclaimed 'near abroad', Russia has consistently demonstrated a propensity to intervene in the affairs of its post-Soviet neighbours. This divergence suggests the existence of a regional paradigm which stands in stark contrast to its declared defence of sovereignty

[5] In line with the insights of the English school of international relations, pluralist notions stand in contrast with solidarist conceptions, emphasizing global governance and shared normative standards, such as democracy and human rights (Allison, 2012; Kaczmarska, 2015).

in other contexts. A particularly perplexing aspect of this dynamic is Russia's selective and instrumental application of international legal principles. Without formally repudiating the tenets of international law, Moscow has positioned itself as its principal interpreter within the post-Soviet space. In this sense, it has maintained a regional 'theatre for contested norms and interpretations of sovereignty, non-intervention, and the use of force' (Allison, 2012: 121; 2020).

Furthermore, Moscow has claimed the role of an arbiter over how neighbouring countries are to be governed and which regions fall under their authority. In essence, Russia has placed a 'shifting value on the sovereignty of neighbouring states relative to the sovereignty claims of their constituent regions, the merits of which can be determined by the Russian government' (Deyermond, 2016: 971). Therefore, Russia's conception of sovereignty appears to be primarily instrumental rather than ideational: while Moscow frequently sets out ideas about state sovereignty, these are employed to advance particular goals 'rather than to develop a consistent position on sovereignty' (Deyermond, 2016: 958).

This differentiation and instrumentality, however, are not phenomena unique to the 21st century; rather, they represent a continuous feature of Russia's approach to Eastern Europe and Central Asia. At their core lies a persistent sense of entitlement over its neighbours. This aspect has attracted growing scholarly attention. Some have highlighted the centrality of ideational narratives in shaping Russia's conception of its sovereignty, particularly its self-perception as a 'great state' (*derzhava*), which is believed to confer privileged rights, reserved for such states (Mälksoo, 2015; Reshetnikov, 2024).[6] In a similar vein, Lewis (2020) underscores the spatial dimension of these narratives, drawing on Carl Schmitt's ideas of *Grossraum* to

6 As Reshetnikov (2024) points out, in Russian discourse, a 'great state' is not identical to a 'great power'.

explain how Russia's identity and foreign policy are shaped (see also Auer, 2015).

A related and increasingly prominent trend is the reframing of Russia's sense of entitlement as a manifestation of imperial nationalism and expansionism, an aspect long minimized, whitewashed or denied by both Russian and Western scholars (Kuzio, 2023). Russian elites and segments of society continue to hold deeply ingrained beliefs in Russia's civilizational supremacy and its right to dominate neighbouring states, translating into resistance to policy change. This perspective has fuelled calls to 'decolonize' Russian studies and to challenge the myth of Russia's 'imperial innocence', a narrative that portrays Russian expansion not as colonialism, but as the organic spread of modernity (Kassymbekova, 2022; Kassymbekova and Marat, 2022; Snyder, 2022; Getka, 2024; Oksamytna, 2024; Sumlenny, 2024).

Undoubtedly, colonialism offers a rich analytical lens for exploring Russia's imperial policies. However, it also carries certain risks. The limited empirical understanding of the specific contexts in which Russian imperial power was exercised, combined with the tendency to import assumptions from Western European colonial experiences, may obscure the long-term, persistent and distinct features of Russian imperialism. These include its evolving ideological, political and legal expressions across the 20th and 21st centuries, as well as its differentiated impact on affected nations and groups. In our view, while studies of Western colonialism offer some valuable comparative insights, they hold limited explanatory power for understanding the continuity and adaptation of Russia's imperial trajectory.

Thus, while we align with many of the insights offered by the aforementioned scholars with deep expertise on Russia and Eastern Europe, we argue that explaining the perplexing features of Russian behaviour since 1991 requires a Russia-centred analytical lens. To this end, we examine Russia's relationship with Ukraine through the prism of the patrimonial model of power. This framework, developed in the extensive work of historian Richard Pipes (1923–2018), posits that Russia adheres to a distinctive patrimonial conception of sovereignty, defined by the fusion between political authority and economic power, and expressed through absolute political authority over territory and its inhabitants (Pipes, 1974). Certainly, a proprietary understanding of royal power was hardly confined to Moscow in the pre-modern era. Yet, in our view emerging during the formation of the Duchy of Muscovy, this patrimonial mindset has endured across centuries, with its core features persisting into the present day (Pipes, 1994; Lynch, 2016; Domanska, 2017, 2019).[7]

While patrimonialism has been used to understand the internal functioning of the Russian state, we draw attention to its external dimensions. Hence, we develop the original concept to emphasize the continuities in Russia's approach to Ukraine and other states, which Russia ruled in the past. The analytical lens of the patrimonial model, where 'the rights of sovereignty and those of ownership blend to the point of becoming indistinguishable' (Pipes, 1994: 23), offers distinctive advantages in understanding Russia's sense of entitlement over Ukraine as central to its patrimony. Moscow has consistently relied on a panoply of shifting and often interchangeable ethno-religious, historical, civilizational and ideological narratives to justify its claims over Ukraine (Van Herpen, 2014; Kuzio,

[7] The patrimonial model has faced extensive criticism, particularly from scholars aligned with the modernization and convergence paradigm, which viewed Russia as a society gradually catching up with Western norms and institutions. This debate was deeply normative, shaped more by scholarly and political divisions within the United States than by the actual nature of the USSR or post-Soviet Russia. While the convergence model has largely been discredited in light of Russia's attack on Ukraine, this shift has occurred with little explicit acknowledgement. Notably, many of its proponents have adopted the 'NATO provocation' argument, thereby reframing Russia's aggression as a defensive response rather than a manifestation of deeper continuities.

2020; Darczewska, 2024). These narratives work in concert to reinforce the underlying patrimonial relationship. Therefore, by centring our analysis on the common thread of historical patrimonial possession, we are able to trace its persistence across time, despite the changing legal and political guises – pre-imperial, imperial, Soviet, and post-Soviet – through which Russia has expressed its claims.

In line with this interpretation, we argue that Russia's conception of its sovereignty is anchored in the self-appointed right to define, absorb and dominate the territories and peoples it considers part of its historical patrimony.[8] This claim to absolute authority within the patrimony is inseparable from the demand that Russia remains unconstrained by external actors or obligations. Accordingly, Russia's prerogative must be recognized and respected by others, a condition portrayed as essential to its sovereignty and great power status. This framework helps explain why any perceived challenge to Russia's control over its neighbourhood is interpreted by the Kremlin as an attack on Russia's sovereignty itself.

The corollary of Russia's entitlement is the belief that the entities deemed part of the patrimony cannot exist independently of their absolute master: they may be granted certain autonomy but always at Moscow's discretion and within the bounds of the patrimony. In this sense, the patrimonial model provides a valuable template for examining the various ways and modalities through which Russia has enacted its control over time. Notably, Moscow has, when expedient, permitted Ukraine's nominal statehood – as during the Soviet period. Similarly, it recognized the nominal sovereignty of its Central and Eastern European satellites between 1945 and 1989. These concessions, however, were considered 'safe', as

[8] In doing this, we are not discussing how exceptional Russia is in those terms or how it compares to other powers in terms of their claims or actions vis-à-vis certain entities, peoples or territories.

Moscow's discretion and the integrity of the patrimony were safeguarded by a network of political, economic and legal instruments embedded within formal Communist union or alliance structures.

Employing a holistic paradigm, such as the patrimonial model, allows us to move beyond attempts to conceptualize limited sovereignty as the lack of independence in the external affairs of the subjugated states. We argue that the distinction between 'internal' and 'external' limitations holds little analytical value, given that Russia's control is premised on the export of a 'clone' political and economic system, such as those installed in Central and Eastern Europe after 1945. Thus, regardless of the 'etiquette of sovereignty' that may be bestowed on some entities, what ultimately matters is Russia's unabridged claim to define the terms of such sovereignty at its discretion, to intervene in order to enforce those terms, or to negate them altogether.

Thus, it is important to emphasize that while this patrimonial mindset has been a constant feature shaping Russia's conduct, its pursuit has been realized in different ways over time. Against this backdrop, our central focus will be on how Russia's policy toward Ukraine was enacted in the post-Soviet period, and how its failure culminated in the large-scale invasion of 2022.

The service of law

The second strand of our analysis adds a critical dimension to understanding how Russia enacted its entitlement over time. We argue that Russia's use of legality has been profoundly expedient and instrumental – serving to underpin, bolster and extend its patrimonial ambitions. By exploring this legalistic approach, we reveal the extent to which legal processes and commitments have been deliberately employed to mask the true intentions behind them. Taking Moscow's legal commitments at face value – as many in the West have been inclined to do – leads to fundamental misconceptions about Russia's aims and the legal tactics it deploys to achieve them. Realists may dismiss this line of inquiry, contending that law is immaterial in so far as it reflects the interests and dominance of powerful states (Steinberg, 2013). This blind-spot is unsurprising, given the expectation that law mirrors the asymmetries of power.

Yet, historically, Russia has placed considerable emphasis on law – both domestic and international – suggesting its significance is far from negligible. We contend that a close study of Russia's use of law is essential to understanding the construction and perpetuation of its patrimonial rule. Within the Soviet system, law performed an essential dual function. First, it created the façade of sovereignty, a legal 'mask' that lent legitimacy to the Communist regime before domestic and external audiences. Second, law served to enforce the political, economic and coercive mechanisms of the Soviet system, thereby supporting the functioning of the patrimonial toolbox. Crucially, under the Soviet law, the patrimonial imperative could override the legal façade whenever necessary.

We build this argument drawing on the work of scholars of the Soviet legal tradition, who have shown that the defining feature of Soviet law was not its lawlessness, but the fusion of legality with arbitrariness and the ability to secure the primacy of the Communist Party rule (Sharlet, 1977; Markovits, 2007; Bækken, 2019; Hendley, 2022). The 'simultaneous repudiation and embrace' of legality was not a mere inconsistency of Soviet law, but a vital part of its political function (Mamlyuk, 2019: 352). Law was – and remains – a political instrument. It is subordinated to the will of the ruler, with its instrumentalism extending to foreign policy as well. Far from ignoring law, Moscow has harnessed it to achieve its goals: in particular, law assumes a pivotal role when the nominal recognition of sovereignty becomes internationally expedient – as was the case after 1945. Admittedly, asserting ideological primacy within the international legal context of relations between the USSR and its Warsaw Pact allies posed significant challenges. Yet aided by the doctrine of Soviet internationalism, Moscow not only managed this tension actively but sought to demonstrate to its Cold War rivals that 'true sovereignty' can only be realized under communism and in union with the USSR (Jones, 1990; Isaeva, 2019).

Thus, Russia developed extensive experience in crafting legal façades and smokescreens. Within the USSR, constitutional legal frameworks became central to perpetuating Russia's dominance over the ostensibly 'sovereign' union republics. Similarly, international law served as a veneer for controlling the satellite states of Central and Eastern Europe. These legacies are crucial for understanding the post-Soviet period, during which Russia's formal recognition of Ukrainian sovereignty should be interpreted not as the genuine abdication of patrimonial claims, but as another iteration of legal masking – a mask that was decisively dropped in 2022.

The post-Soviet patrimonial model and its limits

The patrimonial perspective allows us to frame the conundrum Russia faced in 1991 as follows: having rejected its imperial and Communist past, how was it to preserve its patrimonial rule over Ukraine? We argue that Russia's response to this dilemma involved innovation in tactics but not in essentials. For a range of internal and external reasons, Russia committed to respecting Ukraine's sovereign statehood in 1991. However, this 'etiquette of sovereignty' was bestowed in the confidence that Russia would succeed in asserting its patrimonial rights even in the conditions of Ukraine's formal independence. This was a high-risk strategy.

On the one hand, Moscow was compelled to recognize Ukraine's sovereignty in 1991. The narrative of the republics' sovereignty – however fictional – was already well established. In its effort to disentangle Russia's statehood from that of the USSR, Yeltsin kick-started the 'parade of sovereignties', which ultimately precipitated the collapse of the union (Walker, 2003). As in 1917, the banner of self-determination was raised to dismantle the 'old regime'. In the aftermath, Russia faced profound challenges, which it sought to address by cultivating an image of itself as a new, 'normal' (that is, non-imperial) member of the international system of states. Crucially, Moscow was eager to be recognized as the legitimate inheritor of key Soviet assets – most notably, its nuclear arsenal. To secure this recognition, Russia had strong incentives to demonstrate adherence to international law, including the formal recognition of Ukraine's sovereignty.

On the other hand, Russia's patrimonial toolbox was arguably at its weakest in 1991: Moscow had renounced the use of force, toppled the Communist Party and its apparatus, and dismantled the centralizing levers of the planned economy. Yet, despite the depleted toolbox, the underlying mindset and aims remained unchanged. Moscow operated on the belief that, given the extensive political, economic, religious and ethnic legacies of the tsarist and Soviet periods, Ukraine would be unable to survive independently. In time, Kyiv was expected to return to its 'natural unity' with Russia, be it cloaked in a convenient legal façade.

Drawing on in-depth area studies scholarship of Russia–Ukraine relations since 1991, we demonstrate that this confidence was not entirely unfounded. The unprecedented centralization of the Soviet state had left Ukraine with exceptionally high economic dependence on Russia, while its state capacity to address post-independence challenges was severely underdeveloped. Over the next two decades, Moscow's approach centred on exacerbating this predicament. Russia actively undermined domestic reform efforts to keep Ukraine weak, poor and dependent. Regardless of which political forces came to power in Kyiv, Moscow sought to derail reforms that might reduce Ukraine's reliance on Russia (Sherr, 2006). Simultaneously, Russia exploited Ukraine's economic – and particularly energy – dependence to impose its preferences and maintain leverage (D'Anieri, 1999; Balmaceda, 2013; Wolczuk, 2016).

We argue that legal instruments were central to the success of this post-Soviet set-up. The international agreements between Russia and Ukraine fulfilled the familiar dual function: they conveyed legitimacy while serving Russia's patrimonial interests. In doing so, Russia drew upon the legacy of Soviet legality, where the use of 'vague or ambiguous legal norms … [left] … open a large area of discretionary space which in turn permitted (and even encouraged) arbitrariness' (Sharlet, 1977: 164). Paradoxically, we argue, Russia's turn to international law became a potent mechanism for advancing its interests by capitalizing on Ukraine's craving for independence and its reliance on legal guarantees, particularly those concerning territorial integrity. Much like small states for which 'international law provides a first line of defence' against existential threats (Lupel and Mälksoo, 2019: 5), Ukraine placed considerable trust in international law. Kyiv was also apprehensive that 'unless it adhered strictly to international law, the international community would relegate Russia-Ukrainian relations to an internal "Russian affair", akin to the situation in Chechnya' (Prizel, 1998: 378). However, this reliance proved far from a panacea. As we demonstrate, Moscow adeptly navigated the intricacies and milestones of the treaty-making process (both in terms of process and substance), using Ukraine's vulnerabilities across multiple issues to maximize its leverage and assert control.

Thus, in contrast to the Soviet era, Russia did not overtly condition the recognition of Ukraine's sovereignty on installing a 'clone' or 'friendly' political regime. Nonetheless, the patrimonial logic underpinning Russia's approach necessitated the presence of a pliant leader at the top. Accordingly, the Kremlin actively supported pro-Russian politicians in Ukraine, offering substantial political and financial assistance (Popova and Shevel, 2023; Sherr and Gretskiy, 2023). Conversely, when reform-oriented leaders came to power, Moscow sought to undermine their legitimacy and bolster opposition figures sympathetic to Russian interests.

To a significant extent, Russia's calculus hinged on the prospect of Ukraine's 'autocolonization': the process where a cycle of high dependence drives the elites of a target country to 'seek and accept a diminution in their state's sovereignty' in the hope of receiving various benefits from Russia (Dawisha, 1997: 339). Ukraine's failure to introduce meaningful economic reform, tackle corruption effectively and ensure transparency in governance, facilitated Russia's efforts. For much of the first two decades of independence, the balancing act between private interests and public good came to exemplify the Faustian bargain of Ukraine's leaders with Russia (Bukkvoll, 2004). Despite harbouring deep mistrust of Moscow's intentions, Kyiv pursued engagement with Russia in an attempt to maximize benefits while minimizing commitment (Dragneva and Wolczuk, 2015a). Yet, even when Russia appeared close to controlling Ukraine's leadership, societal mobilization repeatedly disrupted its plans. The mass protests of 2004 and 2014, driven by Ukraine's intrinsic pluralism and political diversity, proved decisive in resisting Moscow's domination (Levitsky and Way, 2002; Hale and Onuch, 2022).

This brings into focus the critical question of the agency exercised by Ukraine: both its political elites and society consistently demonstrated that they were not passive vassals and pawns. Ukrainian fast-changing political developments repeatedly compelled Moscow to recalibrate its tactics, ultimately thwarting its plans. A diverse array of political, societal and cultural dynamics within Ukraine served as the foundation for resistance to Russia's attempts to formalize and sustain its dominance (Hale and Onuch, 2022; Popova and Shevel, 2023).

This stands in stark contrast to Russia's relative success with Belarus's progressive anticolonization under Lukashenka, accelerated after the election fraud and mass protests in 2020. Ukraine's persistent refusal to join Russia-led integration projects – despite considerable pressure – proved a source of frustration for Moscow (Dragneva and Wolczuk, 2015a, 2016). Thus, the final part of our analysis addresses the reasons behind the ultimate failure of Russia's post-Soviet strategy in Ukraine. Faced with repeated setbacks, President Putin resorted to military force, beginning with the annexation of Crimea, followed by the 'limited war' in Donbas in 2014–21, and culminating in the full-scale invasion launched in 2022.

The structure of this book

This book draws on a range of previously disjointed areas of scholarship to craft an interdisciplinary and historically grounded framework to advance the understanding of Russia's evolving relations with Ukraine. In doing so, we deliberately refrain from analysing the full spectrum of narratives and justifications deployed by Russia. Instead, we develop the external dimensions of Russia's patrimonialism, focusing on how Russia has sought to assert control over Ukraine through a combination of legal and extra-legal means. Through this novel perspective we explore Russia's instrumental approach to Ukrainian sovereignty – where law is used as a tool to enact Russia's patrimonial agenda. We conclude that Russia's war on Ukraine and the withdrawal of the 'privilege' of sovereignty in 2022 stem from Moscow's failure to reimpose effective patrimonial control through non-military means. Put differently, the war represents an effort to enforce Russia's entitlement by cancelling 'the etiquette of sovereignty': Ukraine, in this view, can only exist under the auspices of its ultimate sovereign – Russia.

We structure our analysis as follows. Chapter 2 introduces the patrimonial model of power as the pivotal, enduring attribute of Russia's notion of sovereignty. It explains Ukraine's central role in Russia's patrimony and traces Moscow's enactment of this entitlement during the imperial and Soviet periods, with particular emphasis on the instrumental use of law. Chapter 3 examines the period immediately before and after the collapse of the USSR in 1991, during which Russia's patrimonial pursuit appeared to be abandoned in favour of establishing 'normal', inter-state relations with Ukraine. This chapter explores the dilemmas facing Russia's leaders as well as the factors that made President Yeltsin opt for an approach that eventually crystallized as the *post-Soviet* patrimonial model.

Chapters 4 to 6 unpack this post-Soviet model by focusing on three key areas that illuminate Russia's approach: particularly, the interplay and tensions between the nominal recognition of Ukraine's sovereignty and Russia's effort to maintain its patrimonial hold by using its extensive political, military and economic leverage to hollow out Ukraine's sovereignty. Chapter 4 addresses Russia's reluctant recognition of Ukraine's territorial integrity and existing borders in Crimea, and how Moscow retained its military foothold in the peninsula through the continued presence of the Black Sea Fleet. Chapter 5 examines Russia's persistent reluctance to define its land and maritime borders with Ukraine. Then Chapter 6 charts Russia's ongoing attempts to draw Ukraine back into a formal union. Together, these three chapters reveal the key strands of what Moscow hoped would become a tightly woven fabric: its renewed patrimony over Ukraine, exposing the limits imposed on Ukraine's nominal sovereignty.

In doing so, we demonstrate how Moscow used its international agreements with Ukraine to pursue its patrimonial aims. Our findings build on some existing commentary on those agreements and the processes leading to their conclusion, but we offer a new reading of the large set of international accords concluded between (or involving) Russia and Ukraine in the period 1990–2014. This analysis highlights their role in Russia's broader model of controlling Eastern Europe. Faced with Kyiv's limited capacity to resist Moscow's exploitation of its political and economic vulnerabilities, we show how Ukraine was often left reliant on nuanced negotiations and legal drafting, investing in the symbolic weight of such agreements.

Chapter 7 turns to the crisis of Russia's post-Soviet approach, following the Revolution of Dignity in Ukraine in the winter of 2013–14. With its plans thwarted, Moscow escalated its tactics, beginning with the first land grab in Europe since the Second World War and followed by covert military action in Eastern Ukraine. However, we show that this 'limited war' strategy, pursued over 2014–22, ultimately failed to 'coerce Ukraine into friendship' with Russia (Sherr, 2013: 10). Chapter 8 concludes by examining the implications of this failure, culminating in Russia's full-scale invasion of Ukraine in 2022. We argue that Russia's post-2022 options are best understood as the unmasked patrimonial pursuit – where control over Ukraine is claimed through military means – with profound consequences for Ukraine, Europe and the international order, more broadly.

TWO

Russia's Patrimonial Tradition

The idea that Ukraine is not, and has never been, a 'real' state but rather a historical part of the Russian world, lies at the core of Putin's neo-imperial mission (Duben, 2020; Darczewska, 2024; Götz and Ekman, 2024). This mindset, however, is neither recent nor confined to Putin and his closest circle. It reflects Russia's long-standing sense of entitlement over Ukraine, which has been pursued through various means over time, culminating in the open denial of Ukraine's statehood since 2022. To elucidate this dynamic, we draw on the seminal works of the historian Richard Pipes (1923–2018). In his writings, Pipes characterized Russia's conception of sovereignty as shaped by a patrimonial power, which is rooted in the fusion of personal ownership and absolute political authority over conquered territories and peoples.

This patrimonial paradigm – developed under the early Russian rulers – persists up to the present day. It explains the importance of past possession to Russia's modern-day policy toward Ukraine, flanked by a panoply of historical, religious and ethno-civilizational narratives. This paradigm shows why parts of the historical patrimony, such as Ukraine, are regarded as 'an organic part of the "Russian world", without which it becomes an unsustainable entity' (Allan, 2020: 4). Therefore, Moscow's treatment of Ukraine is an enactment of its self-assumed prerogative to determine what 'rights' might be bestowed on entities within its patrimony.

Starting with an overview of Pipes' patrimonial paradigm, this chapter discusses the ways in which Russia expanded and controlled the patrimony during the tsarist and the Soviet periods. We demonstrate how the imperial model of annexation and absorption transformed into the Soviet model of nominal self-determination. Within the Soviet Union, legal façades became fundamental to disguising as well as perpetuating Russia's patrimonial paradigm. Thus, we cast light on the expedient legal framing of the sovereignty of the union republics of the USSR and of its Soviet satellites in Central and Eastern Europe, against the reality of Moscow's patrimonial control.

The tsarist patrimonial model

The patrimonial paradigm

Having emerged and grown outside the world of Western Christendom, Muscovy – by then renamed Russia – joined the European 'Family of Nations' in the 17th century (Mälksoo, 2012). By that stage, it had already developed a distinctive political regime, rooted in the practices of the early Muscovy princes and infused with Byzantine and Mongol elements. Pipes analysed this regime through the lens of Max Weber's concept of the patrimonial system, a variant of personal authority in which 'authority is primarily oriented to tradition but in its exercise makes the claim of full personal powers' (1974: 22). Pipes argued that the term 'patrimonial' aptly describes a regime where 'the rights of sovereignty and those of ownership blend to the point of becoming indistinguishable, and political power is exercised in the same manner as economic power' (1974: 22–23). This proprietary approach to political power distinguished Russia from the West, where authority (*imperium*) was separated from ownership (*dominium*).[1]

[1] Writing in the late 16th century, Jean Bodin, the forefather of the modern theory of sovereignty, spoke of this as a rare and distinctive type of authority, which he defined as 'seigneural' (Pipes, 1974: 65).

We identify and develop three aspects of Pipes' elaboration on the history of the patrimonial system of government in Muscovy. First, the rulers' political mastery over the realm was all-encompassing and unchallenged. It was akin to 'absolute ownership excluding all other appropriation and involving the right to use, to abuse and to destroy at will' (Pipes, 1974: 64). Thus, this right over the patrimony was not – and could not be – subject to any political, legal or economic constraints. The subjects were required to obey the rulers unconditionally, unhindered by any kind of system of reciprocal feudal rights, such as those developed in Western Europe.[2] The prince embodied the state (*derzhava*) which, owing to its divine origin, conferred upon him a power that was 'unlimited, nonrelative, all-pervasive, supreme, undivided, transcendental, and always great' (Reshetnikov, 2024: 72). Within this system, absolute authority would be passed on to the next ruler in sacred trust and with minimum jeopardy to the title.

Second, the internal consolidation of power proceeded hand-in-hand with external expansion. As the power of the omnipotent tsar became ever more entrenched – what Pipes refers to as 'expansion in depth' – sovereignty also came to be defined by an extraordinary degree of territorial acquisitiveness, or 'expansion in breadth' (Pipes, 1974: 118). The prevailing tendency was 'to identify political power with the growth of territory, and the growth of territory with absolute domainial authority' (Pipes, 1974: 84). This created an imperative to acquire territory, which, combined with the absence of natural borders around Muscovy, conferred upon the tsars the prerogative to define the borders of the realm as an essential expression of patrimonial power.

2 The absence of formal limitations on political authority, however, did not mean that it lacked an 'efficient system of political, economic and military organisation … to dispose of the country's entire human and material resources' (Pipes, 1974: 23).

This 'expansion in breadth' evolved into a mission in its own right: '[O]nce an area had been annexed to Moscow … whatever the ethnic and religious affiliation of its indigenous population, it immediately joined the "patrimony" of the ruling house, and all succeeding monarchs treated it as a sacred trust which was not under any circumstances to be given up' (Pipes, 1974: 79). Consequently, once a region was colonized by Russia, its leaders asserted that a claim had been laid, one that could not be challenged by external powers, let alone by the indigenous population asserting their own rights or preferences.

Third, the logic of unlimited patrimonial rule dictated that entities within the patrimony had no subjectivity of their own: their status and right to exist emanated solely from their absolute master (*gosudar*). This logic precluded the toleration of anything beyond expedient, temporary and short-lived political autonomy in the annexed territories. While agreements with local princes or other powers occasionally resulted in the establishment of protectorates or other forms of suzerainty, such arrangements were rare and short-lived.[3] They not were not expressions of the intrinsic rights of the annexed territories and people, but rather the result of a gracious gift or expedient concession by the ruler. Therefore, 'for one reason or another, the privileges granted to conquered people were retracted, contracts were unilaterally abrogated, and the subjects, together with their territories, were incorporated into the regular administration of the Empire' (Pipes, 1954: 3).

In Russia, sovereignty thus embodied its rulers' absolute power over the patrimony, encompassing both the lands and peoples within it. This translated into a perceived right to absorb and dominate territories and populations at the ruler's discretion and in perpetuity. Over time, this prerogative

[3] It is telling that in 1917, the Empire's only protectorates were Finland (as of 1809), Bukhara (1868) and Khiva (1873) (Pipes, 1954: 3–4).

evolved into a mission, one endorsed and facilitated by the nature of the international system that Russia entered at the end of the 17th century, as will be discussed later. As Russia transitioned from a tsardom to a European empire, Western-style reforms influenced certain aspects of the patrimonial regime. Nonetheless, the leaders' absolute power which tolerates no restraint persisted, even if truncated 'behind the façade of the imperial state' (Pipes, 1974: 194), along with the enduring compulsion to expand.

Ukraine and the patrimony

Ukraine has a rich and complex history (Rudnytskyi, 1987; Subtelny, 1981; Velychenko, 1992; Magocsi, 1996; Yekelchyk, 2007; Plokhy, 2015; Hrytsak, 2023). Throughout this history, Russian rule was only one among many encounters with other states; indeed, Ukraine was part of Poland for a longer period than it was part of Russia. However, despite this relatively late encounter, only Russia came to treat the control of Ukraine as an almost axiomatic, historical prerogative (Velychenko, 1992).

Ukrainian territories were initially absorbed into Russia's patrimony through a series of acquisitions during its westward expansion in the 17th and 18th centuries. The first major opportunity arose in 1648, when Cossack Hetman Bohdan Khmelnytskyi staged a Great Revolt against his Polish landlords, resulting in the emergence of an autonomous political formation, the Cossack Host, on both banks of the Dnieper. Unable to secure victory against Poland, Khmelnytskyi sought an ally and, in 1654, signed the Union of Pereieslav with Muscovy. For the Cossacks, the agreement established a military alliance and a protectorate under the authority of the tsar, who in turn pledged to respect certain rights and privileges. For the tsar, however, the agreement signified the acquisition of new subjects and territories, conceived in dynastic terms: 'as far as he and his chancellery were concerned, the tsar was taking over his patrimony' (Plokhy, 2015: 105).

From the tsar's perspective, this was not a contract with his subjects but 'primarily an oath of allegiance, and the fine print just for decoration' (Zygar, 2023: 21).

In 1667, the balance of power in the region led to the division of the Cossack lands between Muscovy and Poland, with only the territories east of Dnieper, known as the Hetmanate, remaining under Russian control. Even though the tsars chipped away at the rights envisaged in the Pereieslav agreement, the Hetmanate developed a distinctive Little Russian (*Malorusy*) identity underpinned by its unique system of government, liberties and rights (Kohut, 1986).[4] Yet, this distinctiveness was soon eroded and the hetman's office was ultimately abolished in 1764 by Catherine the Great as part of her broader project of creating a centralized, rationalized empire. This was followed by the gradual dismantling of the institutions of the Hetmanate, culminating in their full integration into the imperial administrative structures (Kohut, 1988; Plokhy, 2015). With the autonomy of the Hetmanate abrogated, Ukraine was absorbed into the provinces of the Russian Empire. This process was accompanied by extensive efforts to eliminate the cultural and religious distinctions between Ukraine and Great Russia. The Hetmanate elites were gradually assimilated into the imperial structures, with some attaining important and powerful positions. In doing so, they became both subjects and enablers of the Russian imperial expansion, contributing to its transformation into a *European* empire, as will be noted later (Saunders, 1985).

The lands west of the Dnieper, which had remained part of Poland in 1667, were conquered by the Russian Empire only after the partitions of Poland in 1772, 1793 and 1795.[5]

---

4 As Plokhy explains, in the late 16th century 'Little Rus' distinguished the Orthodox lands administered from Kyiv from 'Great Rus' as the Muscovite realm, a religious distinction transferred to the political realm with the Treaty of Pereieslav (2015: 38).

5 Except for Galicia and Bukovina which became part of the Habsburg Empire.

These partitions were initiated by Russia and negotiated with Prussia and the Habsburg Empire. Similarly, a treaty with the Ottomans, signed in Jassy in 1793, sealed the conquest of Crimea and southern Ukraine. Unlike earlier acquisitions, these territories were not granted autonomous status within the empire, which by then had reached its absolutist prime. Instead, they were fully incorporated into the imperial state, with plans for their Russification – slowly but steadily – set in motion (Plokhy, 2017).

In the process, Ukraine became the 'jewel' in Russia's patrimony and increasingly central to the set of historic, religious and ethnic narratives that were developed to define Russia's modern identity. First, Ukraine became pivotal in the construction of the Russian national myth: the idea of an all-Russia nation tracing its origins to Kyiv Rus and thereby uniting Little (Ukraine) as well as White (Belarus) Rus. For the early Muscovy tsars at the height of patrimonial power, ethnicity had not yet acquired political significance (Plokhy, 2015). Accordingly, to the extent that inter-princely arrangements shaped the formation of 9th-century Kyivan Rus, they 'were of the character of an oral distribution of possessions' (Butler, 2020: 11). The link to Kyiv was thus semi-mythological, connecting the tsars to the glory of Byzantium and the Roman Caesars (Zygar, 2023). Muscovite rulers were 'only dimly aware of the history of the Kyivan period, and even less interested in claiming it as their inheritance' (Keenan, 1992: 22). However, in the modern era, the mythology of one nation with a thousand-year history rendered the possession of Ukraine indispensable to the construction of Russia's imperial project.[6] Crucially, the mono-linear and exclusively Russian narrative that Muscovy was the sole legitimate heir to Kyiv Rus

[6] Ironically, the invention of this origin story, attributed to the *Synopsis* of Innokenty Gizel, was not a historical but a diplomatic project, aiming to persuade Muscovy to protect Cossack lands (Plokhy, 2015; Zygar, 2023).

defined the interpretations not only of Russian historiography but also Western interpretations of Russian history (Pelenski, 1992; Kuzio, 2020).

Second, Russia's national mythology became central to its ambitions of transforming into a European power, with the possession of the Western 'borderlands', namely Belarus and Ukraine, serving as evidence of Russia's foothold in Europe (Prizel, 1998). The appropriation of the Kyivan Rus heritage and genealogy thus became the means of Muscovy joining 'the European civilised world' it had previously been excluded from (Mälksoo, 2012). This appropriation conferred upon Russia status as well as special privileges and responsibilities. For Peter the Great, the title of 'All-Rus Emperor' provided a standing comparable to other great European powers, a legacy which subsequent monarchs took even further. By claiming the Kyivan Rus heritage, the Russian Empire positioned itself as one of the oldest and largest states in Europe, thereby asserting parity with its Western peers, such as Britain and France.

Unsurprisingly, Russian imperial historiographers were eager to frame these territorial acquisitions in terms of 'the reunification of Rus', with Catherine the Great 'invoking the historical rights of the Kyivan princes' to legitimize imperial expansion (Plokhy, 2015: 69).[7]

Third, the acquisition of this European Slavic and Orthodox heartland enabled Moscow to claim that Muscovy – renamed Russia – was, at its core, a European Christian civilization. This framing served to contrast Russia with the perceived 'barbarism' and insolence of the populations of the Caucuses and Central Asia, whom Moscow sought to 'civilize' (Hofmeister, 2016;

[7] The effort to back-date the formation of the Russian state was also accompanied by the 19th-century framing of any princely arrangements on the territories of Russia, Belarus and Ukraine as 'constitutional' rather than 'international' treaties, thus subjecting them 'to a different legal regime and not subject to the rules of the law of nations or to analysis under the principles of the law of nations' (Butler, 2020: 11).

Morrison, 2021). This civilizing mission not only justified Russia's continued territorial pursuits but also positioned it as equal and comparable to other European colonial powers.

Thus, by the 19th century, Ukraine's place in the patrimony had become pivotal to Russia's newly constructed historical mythology and national identity. This mythology amplified the traditional conception of sovereignty, which was rooted in the exercise of absolute power over territories and peoples.

The role of (international) law

The modernization of tsarist Russia and the construction of its image as a European power included a nod to 'enlightened legality'. However, this was a veneer that did little to alter the essence of the existing patrimonial regime. Crucially, the empire continued to be held together by the principle of absolute rule and an unlimited monopoly on force. As Bækken observes, Russia 'had plenty of laws, but no *Law*' (2019: 42). Top-down bureaucratic legality served primarily 'to deliver the autocrat's commands to the regions' and 'impose a minimal degree of order across two continents and a highly diverse population' (Pomeranz, 2018: 21).

In practice, this patrimonial system of power was reinforced by the advantages derived from the European legal system, once Moscow learned to 'speak' its language (Mälksoo, 2012). Becoming fluent in international legality enabled Russia to secure non-intervention in its internal affairs, while legitimizing territorial expansion through the law of (just) war, which constituted the normative core of the international system at the time (Cassese, 2012; Glanville, 2013). Acting in concert with other powers, Moscow justified the successive partitions of Poland (1772–95) by invoking the need to contain anarchy and safeguard peace in Europe (Butterwick-Pawlikowski, 2020). Similarly, the right to intervene in defence of Orthodox populations was used to frame its expansion across Moldova, Wallachia and the Caucuses. International audiences largely accepted the narrative that Russia was rescuing people with shared ethnic and religious backgrounds from oppression, even as native elites were either decimated or co-opted, and local populations proselytized.

By 1815, Russia had become one of the key states holding the balance of power in Europe. This privileged position enabled it to apply the rules which served its own needs, disregard those that did not and, when necessary, rewrite others for its own convenience. As a member of the Holy Alliance, Russia was able to impose its will on smaller states, despite the 'dangerous neglect of the principles of international law regarding intervention', and promote a paradigm of differentiated sovereignty (Oppenheim, 1912: §47). Similarly, Russia benefitted from the civilizational wrapping of 19th-century international law, which granted sovereignty to European states while denying it to non-Christian entities (Kleinschmidt, 2016). Indeed, the annexation of lands populated by 'uncivilized' peoples, followed by their Russification, was justified by Russia's elites and leading scholars. First among them was Fyodor Martens, the empire's prominent international lawyer, who championed the civilizing mission with a 'particular intensity and ferocity', exceeding the zeal of 'the arch-imperialists of the time, the British' (Mälksoo, 2012: 778).

In sum, the 19th century marked the golden era of Russian patrimonial expansion. No elaborate legal gymnastics were required to justify Russian territorial acquisition nor its stance toward any national groups, including Ukrainians, within Russia's ever-expanding borders. This was soon to change.

The Soviet federalism model

The Bolshevik revolution of 1917 toppled the imperial system of the Romanovs, rejecting Western capitalist values, law and institutions with vehemence. The Soviet state, which emerged in its place represented a profoundly different ideological, legal, economic and political project. Yet, one fundamental continuity remained: it would be built upon and encompass as much of the former imperial territory as the Bolsheviks could reconquer.[8] While the imperial state collapsed, Russia's patrimonial model persisted – and arguably even flourished – behind the façade of Soviet Marxism-Leninism with its expedient Soviet legality.

The patrimony under threat

The Bolshevik ideology rejected the concept of statehood, viewing it as a capitalist construct rendered obsolete by the emergence of the 'dictatorship of the proletariat'. Following the same logic, national identities were deemed irrelevant in a global proletarian revolution. However, in an instrumental way – in order to undermine tsarist Russia – the Bolsheviks took advantage of the various movements across the empire which were striving toward some form of national self-determination.

As in other parts of the empire, the emergence of the autonomous Ukrainian government heralded the push to self-determination following the demise of the tsarist regime (Hunchak, 1977; Mace, 1983). In June 1917, Ukrainian leaders established the Central Rada and issued a declaration of territorial autonomy, which Lenin initially supported. Similarly, one of the revolutionary government's earliest acts in November 1917, was the Declaration of the Rights of Peoples, which proclaimed the right of all peoples living in the territories of the Russian Empire to be equal and sovereign, including their right to separate statehood and secession. Yet, once in power, the Bolsheviks resisted the fragmentation of the

8 Poland, Estonia, Lithuania, Latvia and Finland escaped from the Bolshevik military attempts to regain the territorial reach of the tsarist empire, something which Stalin sought to remedy two decades later.

patrimony: self-determination was tolerated only insofar as it resulted in the establishment of 'Soviet' governments, which eschewed separation from Soviet Russia.[9]

The period that followed was marked by profound turbulence and destruction, comparable in scale and intensity to the Mongol invasions of the 13th century (Pipes, 1954, 1994). The new challenges required novel solutions to justify the reincorporation of lost territories and further conquest. Moscow launched military campaigns against the Central Rada and its successor governments in Ukraine, which had rejected Bolshevik rule and declared Ukraine's independence. Ultimately, these efforts culminated in the suppression of the so-called Ukrainian Revolution of 1917–21 (Wolczuk, 2001). The Bolsheviks installed a Soviet Ukrainian government, an outcome achieved only on the third attempt in Kharkiv in December 1919.

To fortify Bolshevik rule and its institutions, the Moscow regime was prepared to expand its toolbox and thereby created a new template. This included granting linguistic and cultural concessions in order to co-opt the Ukrainian population, but also providing the façade of Ukrainian statehood (Pipes, 1954; Plokhy, 2017). Indeed, the 1919 Constitution adopted by the Kharkiv government proclaimed the sovereignty of the Ukrainian Soviet Socialist Republic, including its right to conduct an independent foreign policy. Similarly, the December 1920 treaty concluded between the Russian Socialist Federal Sovereign Republic (RSFSR) and Soviet Ukraine recognized Ukraine as a sovereign and independent republic with the right to maintain direct diplomatic relations with other states.

However, these concessions were granted within the context of setting up an economic and military union, in which Russia's

[9] Indeed, the Bolsheviks soon qualified this position with self-determination applying only to 'toiling and exploited people' (Jones, 1990).

ultimate control was clearly evident.[10] Most significantly, behind the formal structures of the 'independent' Soviet Ukrainian government lay the violent and brutal 'pacification' of Ukraine, followed by the imposition of the highly centralized Bolshevik Party system, with pro-independence factions purged once the regime had stabilized (Pipes, 1954). As Plokhy notes, 'The Bolsheviks would "go native" … but they would not allow differences in their ranks concerning the integrity of the state' (2017: 217). Thus, this status of Soviet Ukraine never amounted to genuine independence; rather, it represented a new way to retain Ukraine within the patrimony, with Moscow exercising control across all areas of government, irrespective of Ukrainian needs, aspirations or preferences.

The question of Ukraine's relationship with Moscow came to a head in April 1922, when – contrary to the provisions of the 1920 treaty – the Bolshevik government assumed control over the negotiations with Western powers (Plokhy, 2017). This move provoked protests by several 'independent' Soviet republics, including Georgia and Ukraine. Stalin's proposed solution was to incorporate these republics into Soviet Russia, granting them a nominal autonomous status, while leaving decision-making in the hands of Moscow (Pipes, 1954). Lenin, however, expressed concern that such an overtly imperial arrangement would damage the cause of the world-wide proletarian revolution. After all, one of the Bolsheviks' earliest decrees, had condemned Western colonialism, denouncing 'any incorporation of a small and weak nation into a large

[10] As Sokyrska, Krupenya and Didenko (2021) show, the pronouncements on sovereignty and independence in the preamble of the 1920 Treaty contradicted its contents, which provided for unified government (People's Commissariats) in economic and military matters, with decision-making subordinated to the relevant RSFSR authorities.

and powerful state without precisely, clearly and voluntarily expressed consent'.[11]

To avoid parallels with Western imperialism, Lenin favoured the establishment of a two-tier system of governance, comprising all-Soviet and republican levels. This dual structure created the appearance of the republics' sovereignty within the union. Yet, as Plokhy notes, given the realities of power, the differences were 'more on tactics than on strategy' (2017: 219). Formally, Lenin's model prevailed and a new Union of the Soviet Socialist Republics (USSR) was established. However, this did not signify any relaxation of central control: the federalist arrangement required no substantive revision of Lenin's original position favouring centralism (Szporluk, 2000). This new Soviet-style federal model governing relations between Moscow and its former patrimonial possessions created the legal façade of sovereignty to conceal their de facto reabsorption into the patrimony, as will now be explored.

The republics' sovereignty in law

On the face of it, the USSR was a voluntary union. It was established by Treaty and a Declaration on the Creation of the USSR, which was signed on 30 December 1922 by its four constituent republics: the RSFSR, the Ukrainian Soviet Socialist Republic (Ukrainian SSR), the Belarussian Soviet Socialist Republic (Belarussian SSR) and the Transcaucasian Socialist Federative Soviet Republic. The sovereignty of the union republics was formally expressed through the symbols of statehood, including national executive bodies, constitutions and national emblems and anthems (Walker, 2003).[12]

[11] Decree of Peace, issued by the Second All-Russia Congress of Soviets, 26 October 1917, www.marx-memorial-library.org.uk/sites/default/files/wp-content/uploads/2017/06/5.-Decree-On-Peace-Translation.pdf.

[12] In the same vein, the constitutions of the Ukrainian SSR of 1926, 1937 and 1978 defined Ukraine as a 'sovereign' republic.

Internally, the republics were entitled to exercise 'independent authority' within their territories, whose borders could not be altered without their consent. In 1944, they were also granted external powers, enabling them to enter relations with other states, conclude treaties and participate in international organizations.[13] For the Ukrainian SSR, as for the Belarussian SSR, this external dimension was reinforced by their admission to the UN in 1945, alongside the USSR as a whole. Above all, the sovereignty of the republics was enshrined in their constitutional right to freely exit the Union, as affirmed in the successive Union constitutions of 1924, 1936 and 1977.

This legal picture was reflected in Soviet legal doctrine, which defined republican sovereignty as 'full and unmitigated' and equal to that of the Soviet Union itself (Osakwe, 1985: 713). Accordingly, the official Soviet position maintained that the USSR was a voluntary union of equal and sovereign republics. As such the USSR replaced the imperial policy of absorption and direct rule with a federal system that granted constitutional rights to each republic within the Union. The formula of 'dual sovereignty' not only legitimized Soviet rule domestically. It also enabled Russia to present the Soviet Union as a new, progressive type of state, hence vastly different from Western colonial empires, and the union republics as 'more sovereign' than the constituent units in Western federal countries.

The reality behind the Soviet federalism

Yet, the hollowness of republican sovereignty rendered the aforementioned legal framework largely fictitious. The nominal status of the republics obscured the locus of actual power: the all-union Communist Party, headquartered in Moscow, whose tentacles reached every level of government across the

13 Between 1944 and 1977, this also included the right for the republics to maintain their own military formations.

entire USSR. The Communist Party exercised complete control over public authority, material resources, territories, populations and information flows (Zaslavsky, 1992; Pipes, 1994). This all-encompassing role of the Communist Party was formally confirmed only in the Union's 1977 constitution (Pomeranz, 2018).[14]

Despite the constitutional equality between the constituent republics, Russia's dominance was unmistakable. Russia's institutions were merged with those of the Union, its political elite monopolized leadership positions within the all-union Communist Party and the federal executive, and its cultural and linguistic primacy was systematically reinforced. Moscow's pervasive control was further entrenched through the centrally planned economy, which dictated policy formulation, resource distribution, investment priorities, personnel management, information dissemination and enforcement mechanisms (Williamson, 1993). The capitals of the 15 republics functioned merely as Moscow's administrative extensions, tasked with regional coordination, managing centrally allocated resources and personnel, and implementing the orders issued from the centre.

The centralized nature of the Soviet regime – tightly controlled from Moscow – restricted all aspects of governance within the constituent republics. Central planning reoriented republican economies to serve Soviet planning priorities rather than national needs. Political control was maintained through the appointment of local leaders based on loyalty to Moscow rather than competence or societal support. National and ethnic movements were suppressed through extensive surveillance and coercion. Russification was actively promoted at the expense of republican languages and cultures, while religious suppression remained relentless. As Finkel argues,

[14] Stalin's Constitution of 1936 mentioned the leading role of the Party only in Article 126 dealing with the freedom of association.

these methods were applied in Ukraine with a particular intensity as Stalin regarded 'Ukrainian language and culture as inherently anti-Soviet', unleashing terror, famine and repression to turn it into a 'model republic' and a 'bastion of Moscow-based Soviet power' (2024: 8).

The Soviet federal model thus concealed the effective continuation of Moscow's control over the patrimony. Similarly, the ideological fervour of the proletarian revolution, despite its gradual dilution, masked the old imperial habits of territorial expansion: the conquest of the Baltics, a sizeable part of Finland and Bessarabia as well as western Ukraine and Belarus in 1939–40 were justified as the liberation of the masses from oppression.[15] These acts of expansion followed a consistent pattern: Moscow would invade, install a Soviet-controlled government, which would then call for absorption into the Soviet Union. It is hard to contest the conclusion that Stalin's 'colonialist mindset and exploitative ambitions … must have echoed the deepest sins of capitalist great powers in the eyes of many devout communists' (Reshetnikov, 2024: 188).

Once incorporated into the Soviet Union, the newly conquered territories were absorbed into a complex, multi-layered system of national-administrative units, which allowed considerable scope for arbitrary decision-making. Depending on political expediency, these territories could be elevated to the status of 'sovereign republics' or downgraded to 'autonomous' entities. Their autonomy could be expanded when convenient or revoked entirely. A notable example is the Crimean Autonomous Soviet Socialist Republic, which was dissolved in 1945 following the mass deportation of the Crimean Tatars in 1944. At times, even the pretence of a union of republics was abandoned. Khrushchev's proposal to transform the USSR into a unitary

[15] Moscow rationalized its actions with a plethora of arguments, including self-defence and 'progressive intervention' against Nazi as well as capitalist rule (Rostow, 1981).

state – on the grounds that borders had become irrelevant as life was 'organised on a single socialist foundation' – reveals the virtually unlimited extent of Moscow's power and underscores the myth of republican sovereignty (Walker, 2003: 37).

The instrumentality of Soviet law

The Soviet patrimonial model depended on the supremacy and unity of the Communist Party, as well as the Soviet central planning and repression apparatus. Nevertheless, law played a pivotal role in sustaining and legitimizing the system. Indeed, the initial rejection of law, the dismissal of 'sovereignty' as a bourgeois construct, and the anticipated withering away of the state – core tenets of Marxist-Leninist doctrine – soon gave way to the pragmatic demands of Soviet rule (Jones, 1990; Markovits, 2007; Pomeranz, 2018).

The instrumental use of law in the USSR manifested in two principal ways. First, constitutional law provided the cover of republican sovereignty for both domestic and international audiences, lending a veneer of legitimacy to the Communist state. Second, Soviet legality facilitated patrimonial control by enforcing its mechanisms through an extensive network of legal rules and institutions across all branches of domestic law. In this framework, law imposed no constraints on state power, leaving the party-state bureaucracy effectively beyond its reach. Any divergence between the will of the leadership and the formal provisions of law were resolved through the principle of *partiinost*, which ensured that the directives of the Communist Party prevailed over any legal niceties. As Hendley observes, 'formal law was not literally ignored … but stretched' to accommodate even acts of terror (2022: 214).

In most areas of law, the scope for arbitrary action was maximized through ambiguity and vagueness in legal drafting (Sharlet, 1977). For instance, with regard to the competences of the republics, the powers of the federal government were broadly and poorly defined, thereby reinforcing centralized control (Smith, 1985). As a result, Soviet constitutions offered few substantive guarantees of rights or prerogatives to the republics: there existed no mechanism to implement key constitutional rights of the republics, such as the right to secede from the Union. Similarly, beyond its association with 'the omnipotence of power within certain territory', sovereignty conveniently remained an underdeveloped notion in Soviet legal and political theory, with the term itself often avoided in favour of new propagandist slogans (Antonov, 2012: 99).

Accordingly, under Soviet-style legality, any expression of republican autonomy could be suppressed as an anti-Soviet act. As Bilinsky summed up:

> The 1977 Soviet constitution did not abolish the Union Republics, nor did it deprive them of the formal right to secession. But … it provided for a more centralised government and, on closer legal analysis, its paragraphs appear more compatible with the outright abolition of the Union Republics than even with traditional Soviet pseudo-federalism. (1992: 167)

However, this pseudo-federalism ultimately sowed the seeds of its own demise. As Pipes prophetically observed, 'this purely formal feature of the Soviet Constitution may well prove to have been historically one of the most consequential aspects of the formation of the USSR' (1954: 285–286).

The Soviet internationalism model

The conceptions of sovereignty and Soviet legality were similarly deployed in an instrumental way to frame Moscow's control over the Central and Eastern European states at the end of the Second World War. The liberation from Nazi Germany provided the opportunity for the Red Army to ensure further expansion into Europe. As Pipes observed, following the war, the Soviet Union stood as the sole imperial power that not only 'refused to give up the colonial acquisitions made by its "feudal" and "bourgeois" predecessors', but also succeeded in 'increasing them by the addition of new dependencies in Eastern Europe and the Far East' (1980: 358).

Unwilling to settle for a mere 'sphere of influence', Stalin considered incorporating these states into the USSR using the familiar method of exporting a 'clone' regime and engineering a 'voluntary union'. He ultimately abandoned the plan for incorporation, recognizing the potential damage to the USSR's carefully cultivated international image as a champion of anti-imperialism, the domestic costs of absorption, and the risk of renewed confrontation with the West (Jones, 1990).

Consequently, the Central and East European states were allowed to retain formal sovereignty and statehood as 'people's republics', a status reflected in their national constitutions (Rakowska-Harmstone and Gyorgy, 1979). In practice, however, this sovereignty was a legal fiction premised on Russia's effective patrimonial control. Having exported Soviet-style governments to these states, Moscow relied on the familiar model of subordination to the Communist Party, which functioned as a 'form of proprietorial rights system' (Jones, 1990: 57). Control was further entrenched through the economic dependencies created by the Soviet economic model and, above all, through the persistent presence of Soviet military forces stationed across their territories (Bideleux and Jeffries, 2007; Applebaum, 2012). As Jones aptly notes, 'Soviet hegemony was so strong that the Soviets could formally bestow upon the bloc states the "blank cheque" of formal sovereignty, without fear that it will be drawn' (1990: 113).[16]

Therefore, as the veneer of legality remained important, relations between the USSR and the satellite states were structured

[16] However, even if nominal, the existence of separate statehood provided an inspiration and exerted a powerful impact on the independent movements in the Soviet Union, as appreciated by some scholars, even well before the collapse of the Warsaw Pact (Szporluk, 1976).

on an *inter-state* basis, governed by international agreements and aligned with the tenets of the newly established UN. However, in essence, there was a 'fundamental incompatibility at almost every point between traditional Communist doctrine and the principles of the UN Charter' (Gardner, 1964: 845). Sustaining the Soviet patrimonial model within the framework of international law thus required a new form of legal manoeuvring. The existing formula of conquest and absorption, either openly (under tsarism) or under the cover of federalism (under communism) was no longer directly applicable. In sum, neither Russian imperial nor early Soviet practices offered a viable template for maintaining patrimonial control in the context of internationally recognized state sovereignty in Central Europe (Jones, 1990).

This required a novel arrangement. Soviet political and scholarly doctrine resolved the conundrum by framing relations between socialist states as a 'new type' of proletarian internationalist relations, and thus, a distinct subcategory of general international law (Osakwe, 1972). Accordingly, the Soviets did not formally reject the principles of sovereignty, non-interference and sovereign equality, but rather qualified them. Specifically, it was argued that socialist internationalism required socialist states to transcend general international law in their mutual relations to foster friendly and peaceful cooperation. Indeed, the USSR viewed the East European regional system as an extension of the Soviet 'family of nations' (Rakowska-Harmstone and Gyorgy, 1979: 4). This framework imposed special rights and obligations on socialist states, including the duty to pursue close economic cooperation in the service of the construction of socialism. This rationale underpinned the socialist economic integration model, which sustained the economic levers of the Soviet patrimonial model (Butler, 1971).[17]

[17] This cooperation was formalized through the structures of the Council of Mutual Economic Assistance which existed from 1949 until 1991.

More significantly, the same logic was used to justify Soviet military interventions, notably in Hungary in 1956 and in Czechoslovakia in 1968.

In essence, Moscow positioned itself as the ultimate arbiter of which 'foreign governments could be tolerated and which should be opposed and overthrown' (Kennan, 1961: 189), by military means if necessary. This principle was formalized in the so-called 'Brezhnev Doctrine', which asserted that 'the sovereignty of each socialist country cannot be set up in opposition to the interest of the socialist world and the world revolutionary movement' (Kovalov, 1968). The notion of 'limited sovereignty' of the socialist states thus granted the Soviet leadership the right to intervene in other communist countries to suppress both perceived external threats and any internal deviations from the Soviet model of communism (Rostow, 1981).

In a masterclass of legal manipulation, Moscow asserted that socialist internationalism represented the true fulfilment of the principles of international law. Therefore, 'by encroaching upon the mainstays of socialism, the counter-revolutionary elements in Czechoslovakia undermined the very foundations of the country's independence and sovereignty', while Soviet intervention was portrayed as an act of friendship aimed at safeguarding those foundations (Kovalov, 1968).

This rationalization of sovereignty in the context of socialist internationalism raised the question whether it constituted a distinctive 'Soviet international' branch of international law or merely the construction of a set of 'socialist principles of international relations' (Butler, 1971; Osakwe, 1972). Regardless of the verdict on this, it is evident that Moscow constructed a regional international order that reinforced its role as the guardian of the communist realm, instrumentalizing law whenever it conflicted with Soviet interests (Jones, 1990). In effect, Soviet legality provided Moscow with broad latitude to exercise control over its extended dominion.

Conclusions

Notwithstanding the pronounced discontinuities between the tsarist empire and the Soviet Union, the patrimonial mentality at the core of Russia's conception of statehood and sovereignty endured. For Moscow, the right to absorb lands – including Ukraine – and determine the fate of their populations remained an unquestioned prerogative. While political leaders were willing to grant varying degrees of autonomy for reasons of political expediency, whether domestic or international, such flexibility never compromised Moscow's overarching control over its patrimonial possessions. Thus, although Ukraine was formally elevated from an imperial province to a 'sovereign' Soviet republic, the change in its actual autonomy – political and economic – was largely nominal. It was still ruled by Moscow.

The USSR was a 'unitary, centralised, totalitarian state' of a kind the tsarist state had never been (Pipes, 1954: 285), yet the legal fiction of sovereignty was central to the construction of the Soviet patrimonial model. Therefore, it is one of history's ironies that the legal façade that obscured where true power lay for 70 years, was ultimately turned against the Soviet centre by the republican capitals (Walker, 2003). The Communist system began to unravel under the weight of its own political, social and economic contradictions and failures, despite Gorbachev's efforts to reform the model in the late 1980s.

As Ukraine opted for independence for a second time in the 20th century, Russia once again confronted the prospect of losing a pivotal part of its patrimony. With the collapse of Communist Party rule and the dissolution of the Soviet Union, the levers of power previously concealed behind the façade of Soviet pseudo-federalism and Soviet internationalism could no longer be relied upon. Consequently, in 1991 Moscow had limited means to prevent the disintegration of the patrimony without resorting to military force and widespread bloodshed, as it had during the Ukrainian Revolution of 1917–21.

Suddenly, the Kremlin faced the challenge of developing a new model to preserve an empire that had been in the making for over four centuries. Yet, it possessed ample experience and instruments to deploy in the post-Soviet context. As subsequent chapters will argue, Moscow's treatment of the satellite states, characterized by formal recognition of sovereignty while effectively nullifying it under the guise of international law, served as a useful model for its relations with the post-Soviet states.

THREE

The End of the USSR and the Search for a Post-Soviet Patrimonial Model

The period leading up to and immediately after the collapse of the USSR left the political elite in Moscow scrambling to deal with three interconnected challenges. These were: first, how to manage the dissolution of the Union, second, how to address the power vacuum in Moscow following the implosion of the Communist Party, and, finally, how to retain control over Ukraine. As pointed out by Oleg Rumyantsev, head of the constitutional committee of the Russian parliament, '[T]he Soviet Union was a form of existence of Russia' (cited in Zubok, 2021: 366). Thus, these were existential issues for the new Russian rulers. The conundrum for Russia, and in particular Yeltsin, who increasingly had the initiative in Moscow, was how to achieve these objectives while adhering to his very public commitments to respect Ukrainian sovereignty.

Moscow's subsequent approach to Ukraine indicates that the early 1990s did not end the patrimonial paradigm, regardless of any public rhetoric or agreements to the contrary. This chapter examines Russia's manoeuvring to recognize Ukraine's sovereignty yet retain it within its patrimony, starting with an overview of the run-up to the collapse of the Soviet Union. We show that Russia sought to establish a new, reformed union to enable its continued domination. Yet, this plan was scuppered by Ukraine's opposition, forcing Moscow to conduct relations with Ukraine on the basis of international law and in the framework of inter-state relations.

Thus, Russia nominally rejected its imperial and Soviet pasts, eschewing forced reabsorption in the process. Yet the acceptance of Ukraine's independence was an expedient, unmistakably conditional and temporary measure, signalling the beginning of a new phase in Russia's patrimonial control.

Rocking the Soviet model

The nominal sovereignty of the Soviet republics had little substantive meaning in the centralized political and economic structure of the Soviet system (see Chapter 2). However, the launch of Gorbachev's *perestroika* in the late 1980s inadvertently opened the floodgates for the articulation of the long-suppressed national aspirations across the Union. This led to demands to realize the constitutional status of the union republics as sovereign states (Roeder, 1991). Led by developments in the Baltics, the concept of sovereignty – albeit vaguely and ambiguously defined – became the banner for broad political mobilization across the Soviet republics, including Ukraine (Kuzio and Wilson, 1994; Walker, 2003).

Yet, the efforts to transform the legal façade of the Soviet model into reality exposed its inherent contradictions. The republics' assertions of supremacy over their own laws and claims to control of assets within their territories, alongside demands to activate the previously meaningless right to exit the Union, posed a direct challenge to the very foundations of the system. Although outright secession was not initially envisaged, none of these demands could be accommodated without an entirely new settlement on the status of republics, if the Union was to survive.[1]

1 The Baltic republics' course soon became more determined, with Lithuania leading the way and declaring full independence from the USSR in March 1990.

In an effort to counteract the growing centrifugal and separatist tendencies, the Soviet leadership sought to preserve the Union by tweaking its legal façade. In April 1990, Gorbachev introduced a package of federal laws implementing the principle that 'without a strong union there can be no strong republics' (Walker, 2003: 71).[2] However, this policy of top-down, nominal reform proved unsustainable and in June 1990, Gorbachev took the fateful decision to start work on a new Union treaty as the basis for a renewed federation.[3]

Gorbachev's hand was forced by Yeltsin, who made Russia's sovereignty the focus of his campaign for leadership of the Russian legislature in May 1990. On 12 June 1990, Yeltsin secured overwhelming support for the Declaration of Sovereignty of the RSFSR, skilfully mobilizing a wide coalition of nationalists, democrats and mass populists. Yeltsin promoted 'sovereignty' as the means of ending the perceived injustice of Russia's existing relationship with the Soviet centre and tackling its mounting economic problems, thereby restoring 'Russian greatness'.[4] Accordingly, the 1990 Declaration referred to sovereignty as the 'natural and necessary precondition for the existence of Russia's statehood' (Para 2) and asserted the legislative and economic supremacy of the

---

[2] This package included laws on delineation of powers as well as secession, but in effect made the latter impossible. Further, these measures did little to change the fundamental levers of Soviet patrimonial control, such as the Soviet ministries' control over all assets deemed of all-union importance.

[3] Gorbachev's plan for a treaty drafted by an expert group and closely controlled by the centre did not survive the dynamics of negotiating with the leaders of the republics who agreed to participate in the process (Walker, 2003).

[4] Russia was seen to carry the economic burden of the USSR as a whole, while – formally even if not in reality – having limited input in the decisions over its fortunes taken by the Soviet leadership given that it lacked its own Russian ministries or a republican branch of the Communist Party.

Russian authorities within the RSFSR's territory. This was a distinctly political project: Yeltsin was not 'the slightest bit interested in a precise legal definition of the meaning of sovereignty – far more important was its political effect in putting Gorbachev and the central leadership on the defensive' (Walker, 2003: 80).

The 1990 Declaration's reference to a 'reformed USSR' rather than some kind of separation of Russia from the Union signalled a renewal rather than a rejection of Russia's dominant role within the Union. It marked a revision of Russia's relations with the Soviet centre rather than a withdrawal from it. The challenge was neatly summarized by Russia's well-known political scientist Tsipko: 'Moscow cannot secede from Moscow. … This is unnatural, it is madness' (cited in Solchanyk, 1992: 33). For many in Russia, the Soviet Union and Russia remained indistinguishable entities.

Yeltsin opposed Gorbachev on many issues and adopted an anti-communist, pro-democratic and pro-reform position, but he also favoured a union. Being anti-Soviet and anti-Gorbachev did not mean being anti-union. Yet, Yeltsin steered an ambiguous – and frequently inconsistent – political course.

On the one hand, Yeltsin actively participated in the negotiations on a new union treaty led by Gorbachev, the so-called Novo-Ogarevo process, emphasizing Russia's commitment to the initiative. His cooperation helped sustain the process, delivering three consecutive drafts of the treaty by August 1991. For Yeltsin, the bonus was that the negotiations were an effective way of extracting concessions from the centre and strengthening the positions of the republics.

On the other hand, Yeltsin simultaneously undermined many of Gorbachev's initiatives. For example, in response to the Soviet Union's failed economic reforms during the summer of 1990, he adopted a series of unilateral measures aimed at increasing Russia's direct control over its economic institutions and policies. These failures reinforced Yeltsin's belief that the federal authorities were incapable of addressing Russia's fundamental problems.[5] To strengthen his position vis-à-vis Gorbachev, Yeltsin pursued horizontal alliances with other republics. To this end Yeltsin engaged in direct bilateral relations, most notably with Ukraine, expressing support for its sovereignty, as will be discussed later, and defended Lithuania following the Soviet hardline crackdown of pro-independence forces in January 1991. Moreover, Yeltsin viewed Gorbachev's proposed referendum on the future of the USSR, scheduled for March 1991, as a threat to Russia's sovereignty project. He strategically co-opted the referendum campaign to garner popular support for the creation of the Russian presidency (Zubok, 2021).

All this manoeuvring, however, was undertaken in the confidence that – with or without Gorbachev – the union between Russia and Ukraine would be preserved. Ukraine's cautious approach to sovereignty, which remained vaguely defined until the autumn of 1991, stood in contrast to the firm opposition to the new union treaty negotiations expressed by Moldova, Georgia and Armenia, not to mention the Baltic states. This difference suggested that Yeltsin's assumptions were not entirely unfounded.

Ukraine's awakening

The national movement in Ukraine, growing in confidence, saw Gorbachev's policy of *perestroika* (restructuring) as an existential opportunity and seized it. By 1989, calls for Ukrainian sovereignty emerged from both the so-called national communists, disillusioned by Moscow's handling of the Chernobyl disaster, and the national democrats, who

5 These steps led to the so-called 'war of laws' of late 1990, but had a limited effect given the structural fundamentals of the system, such as the control exercised by Soviet ministries.

sensed an opportunity for historical justice (Plokhy, 2015). Russia's Declaration of Sovereignty in June 1990 was swiftly followed by Ukraine's own Declaration of Sovereignty on 16 July 1990. This step was also seen as a prerequisite for Ukraine's participation on equal terms with Russia in the negotiations on the new union treaty announced by Gorbachev (Matlock, 1995).

The Ukrainian declaration, like its Russian counterpart, asserted 'supremacy over all its territory' and independence in 'determining any issue of its state affairs'.[6] However, it went further in key respects. Following the lead of the Baltics, Ukraine claimed sovereignty in cultural, economic and security matters as well as in international relations. Notably, the declaration made no direct reference to the USSR, except to stipulate that any new union agreement would be informed by the principles of the declaration. In other words, independence was neither explicitly endorsed nor ruled out.

Ukraine's newly elected leader, Leonid Kravchuk, steered a cautious path toward sovereignty. He participated in the drafting of a new treaty to reform the USSR under Gorbachev's leadership, while simultaneously working with Yeltsin to maximize republican autonomy. Yet, even before the first draft of the treaty was published, Ukraine's position hardened. Kravchuk, attuned to the political significance of the student protests in Kyiv in September 1990, known as the 'revolution on granite' (Kowal et al, 2020), responded by implementing one of the students' key demands. Accordingly, the Ukrainian Supreme Soviet declared that it would be premature to conclude a union treaty before completing state-building and adopting a new constitution (Solchanyk, 1996). This last condition – the adoption of a new constitution

6 https://static.rada.gov.ua/site/postanova_eng/Declaration_of_State_Sovereignty_of_Ukraine_rev1.htm

before signing any treaty – rendered Ukraine's participation in a new union a distant prospect and one to be decided in Kyiv rather than in Moscow (Wolczuk, 2001).

Ukraine's extreme caution stemmed not only from distrust of the Soviet centre but also from concerns about Russia's intentions for the new Union. Kyiv sought a genuine and unconditional Russian commitment to recognizing Ukraine' sovereignty, sovereign equality and territorial inviolability as the foundation for any new framework. Ukrainian parliamentarians attempted to build support for this cause in Moscow by appealing to Russia's democrats (Solchanyk, 1996). Kyiv also pushed for Russia's assurance regarding respect for existing borders and national sovereignty during the negotiations of the bilateral Friendship and Cooperation Agreement (FCA) of November 1990. This was to no avail, despite Yeltsin's pledge: 'I categorically reject the accusation that Russia is now claiming some special role. … Russia does not aspire to become the centre of some new empire. It does not want to have an advantage over other republics' (Solchanyk, 1996: 25). Boris Tarasiuk (1996), a Ukrainian official and later Foreign Minister of Ukraine, expressed concern that Russia's focus during the FCA negotiations was on securing Ukraine's cooperation against the Soviet centre, without offering unconditional guarantees on sovereignty. Ultimately the final agreement referred only to 'the territorial integrity of the Ukrainian SSR and RSFSR inside the borders presently existing within the framework of the USSR'. This linkage between Ukraine's territorial integrity and the preservation of a union would prove pivotal in Russia's future dealings with Kyiv, as discussed in Chapters 4 and 5.

Gorbachev's call for a referendum on the Union in March 1991 offered Kyiv an opportunity to seek popular support for its course. Kravchuk added a supplementary question: 'Should Ukraine be a part of a union of soviet sovereign states on the basis of the Declaration of State Sovereignty of Ukraine?'

To this, 81 per cent of voters responded affirmatively.[7] This outcome gave Kyiv further room to manoeuvre. Ukraine remained engaged in the Novo-Ogarevo process, but as the talks inched toward completion, its parliament declared that the June 1991 draft union treaty was a mere basis for discussion. It also appointed a commission to assess the treaty's compatibility with the Declaration of Sovereignty, with a report due in September 1991 – after the planned signing date of 20 August 1991.

Thus, by mid-August 1991 Ukraine appeared set – be it conditionally – to join the reformed Union.[8] However, the hardliners' coup in Moscow on 19 August 1991 against Gorbachev and the new treaty threw everything into disarray. Two days after the coup collapsed, Ukraine declared independence, subject to confirmation by referendum scheduled for 1 December 1991. The full implications of the Declaration of Independence on 24 August were not immediately clear. The document expressed the intent to establish Ukraine as an 'independent democratic state', invoking its 'thousand-year state tradition' and its right to self-determination.[9] Yet, the declared secession from the USSR did not preclude Ukraine's membership in a reformed union, whether led by the existing centre or formed through horizontal arrangements among republics.

[7] This step undermined the effect of Gorbachev's question, 'Do you consider it necessary to preserve the Union of Soviet Socialist Republics as a renewed federation of equal sovereign republics, which will fully guarantee the rights and freedoms of all nationalities?', which received 70.2 per cent.

[8] As Walker (2003) argues, the August 1991 draft suffered from poor design. It was based on the continuity of the Soviet paradigm of dual sovereignty (see Chapter 2), an unsatisfactory solution aggravated by the significant gaps in drafting. On this basis, signing the treaty would hardly have been a done deal.

[9] https://static.rada.gov.ua/site/postanova_eng/Rres_Declaration_Independence_rev12.htm

Over the following months, Ukraine's position became more defined. Kravchuk met with Gorbachev in early September 1991 to discuss the new treaty, in case the 24 August declaration was not approved at the referendum. However, Kravchuk insisted that Ukraine would only consider joining a confederation, not a more binding federation (Plokhy, 2014). In October, the Ukrainian parliament voted to suspend participation in such negotiations until after the referendum. Ukraine began to boycott the Soviet centre, freezing interactions with all-Union Soviet institutions in Moscow.[10] The referendum on 1 December showed overwhelming support for independence across all regions of Ukraine. Following his election as president on the same day, Kravchuk announced that he would not sign any union treaty premised on central government or authority. This decision was formalized by a parliamentary resolution on 5 December 1991, effectively ruling out membership in any union that compromised Ukraine's independence.

The shock of Ukraine's independence

The Ukrainian declaration was widely interpreted in Moscow as a 'stab in the back' and a decisive step toward the uncontrolled disintegration of the Union. Yet, 'uncontrolled' in this context signified a potential paradigm shift: the prospect of the 'brotherly' Ukrainians choosing to forge an independent path. The resulting psychological impact was profound – so much so that Yeltsin instructed his press secretary, Pavel Voshchanov, to threaten Ukraine with territorial revision should it leave the Union.[11]

10 Ukraine showed interest only in the Treaty on the Economic Community concluded on 18 October 1991. Notably, however, it signed it only in November under some pressure from the West that they would receive less aid and investment (Walker, 2003).

11 Yeltsin subsequently distanced himself from this announcement.

The near-immediate emergence of territorial revision threats underscored the conditional nature of the 1990 bilateral FCA. More significantly, it exposed Russia's deep-seated sense of patrimonial entitlement over Ukraine and its territories. Voshchanov's statement referenced territories that might be considered legally contentious within the framework of the USSR, such as Crimea, aligning with the narrative of Ukraine's artificial construction as a Soviet republic. However, the list also included Donbas and segments of southern Ukraine, which had never belonged to the RSFSR. This suggested that post-Soviet Russia was now invoking its imperial tsarist heritage. In effect, alongside calls from Russian nationalists to reclaim territories with sizeable ethnic Russian populations, the new leadership in Moscow introduced an entirely new reference point, the Russian Empire, to discuss Ukraine's drive to independence.[12] According to Voshchanov, Yeltsin was determined to place Ukraine in its 'rightful place', meaning 'in the Union, together with Russia and under its control' (Plokhy, 2014: 179).

The statement provoked protests in Ukraine and drew criticism from both Russia's democrats and the West. The parliamentarians dispatched by Yeltsin to defuse the situation failed to persuade the Ukrainians to halt the move toward independence. The talks merely reaffirmed the principles of the 1990 FCA, including its – albeit conditional – respect for sovereignty, even though for the first time, the USSR was referred to as 'former'. This outcome was far from what Yeltsin had intended. Unlike the Baltic states, whose independence Moscow had recognized without conditions or intimidation – despite their sizeable Russian minorities – Ukraine was not to be 'let go' as easily (Plokhy, 2014). Nonetheless, the talks bought Moscow some time: the joint communiqué emphasized the need for coordinated

[12] In the press conference, Voshchanov also referred to Kazakhstan, leading to parallel talks to placate the Kazakh elite.

efforts to prevent uncontrolled disintegration, and called for the establishment of interim state structures for a transitional period.[13]

Russia now faced the real prospect of Ukrainian independence should the referendum confirm this course, a scenario for which it was politically and psychologically unprepared. At the same time, Yeltsin's own position in Moscow became increasingly vulnerable. While he had previously benefitted from divisions between communists and reformers, between nationalists and unionists, these fault lines did not apply in the case of Ukraine. It was no longer clear whom he could rely on. As Tsipko (1991) observed, Yeltsin's predicament was acute: he could either embrace independence – Ukraine's as well as Russia's – or seek to preserve the Union, potentially at the cost of his victory over the centre. The Russian political elite grew restless, awaiting a resolution, as Yeltsin's leadership on Ukraine and the broader 'Union question' came under increasing scrutiny.[14]

In the autumn of 1991, an informal coalition of communists, nationalists and reformers emerged in opposition to Ukraine's independence. Committed to preserving the Union at all costs, they advocated for a hardline stance on Kyiv – either to prevent a vote for independence in the referendum or, failing that, to undermine its validity. For instance, Gorbachev's adviser Shakhnazarov argued that, with respect to Crimea, the Donbas and Southern Ukraine: 'It should be stated plainly and clearly, without constraint, that those regions are historical parts of Russia, and it does not intend to renounce them if Ukraine should wish to cease being part of the Union' (cited in Plokhy, 2014: 259). Similarly, the

---

13 'The Ukraine: It had to be stifled immediately', *Nezavisimaya Gazeta*, 31 August 1991, *Current Digest of the Soviet Press*, XLIII: 35, p 15.

14 The lack of vision and leadership was on full display as Yeltsin left for a long holiday, returning to full-time action only in the middle of October.

former dissident and Nobel laureate Alexander Solzhenitsyn contended that the referendum results should be counted region by region, asserting that Ukraine as a whole was not a legitimate entity (Solchanyk, 1996). Vice President Rutskoy issued a direct warning against Ukraine's defiance in dealing with Moscow, citing Russia's possession of nuclear weapons (Kozyrev, 2019: 77).

There was similar unease among reformers. While some welcomed a degree of independence for Russia as a means of reducing its economic burden, they still favoured a union under Moscow's leadership – even if as a looser arrangement based on market relations.[15] Concerned about the potential replication of the Yugoslav scenario on a much larger scale, they also cautioned against extreme nationalist ambitions. Others, such as Yeltsin's Secretary of State Genady Burbulis, argued that Russia was the 'sole republic that could and should be a successor to the Union and its structures', including its nuclear arsenal and the UN seat (Zubok, 2021: 366). As Zubok notes, such a succession formula implied that other republics would have to negotiate their independence *with Russia*. However, this approach was deemed risky, as it reinforced perceptions of Russia's imperial ambitions and complicated talks with Ukraine over the parameters of the new, more horizontal union or confederation that Moscow was hoping to establish. Ultimately, the proposal reflected the belief that Ukraine's independence could not be determined by the Ukrainians alone, but would have to be granted by Russia – on its own terms.

Nonetheless, all forces seemed to be united by the conviction that economic interdependence would, in time, lead to Ukraine's inevitable reintegration with Russia. As

15 Additionally, the much-needed reform of Russia's own economy would not be hindered by countries in which communist elites were still entrenched.

the dissident Yelena Bonner remarked: '[W]e are all bound together economically, and no sort of national independence will be able to sever these ties.'[16] Similarly, there was a prevailing belief that any concessions made by Russia to the other republics, would be temporary. Burbulis argued that after Russia had rebuilt its statehood and was back on its feet, 'everyone will gravitate towards it, and it will be possible to rearrange everything' (cited in Zubok, 2021: 365). At that point, any thorny issues could be revisited: 'One day we might be able to revisit the fate of, say, Crimea, but only if today we discussed building democracy and friendship in both countries and avoided creating hostility by making territorial claims' (Kozyrev, 2019: 43). Overall, despite seemingly radical disagreements among Russia's political factions regarding Ukraine, these differences were about strategy rather than substance. The shared underlying assumption was that Ukraine remained part of Russia's patrimony, and its independence – if acknowledged – was to be conditional and reversible.

Recognizing Ukraine

In the autumn of 1991, Yeltsin aligned himself with the reformist lobby, appointing its members to senior positions within the RSFSR government. His priorities were twofold: to launch radical economic reforms and to secure Russia's inheritance of the USSR, along with the Western endorsement for this claim (Zubok, 2021). The course still involved cooperation with Gorbachev on a new treaty, advocating for some form of a confederation – an arrangement he hoped would be palatable to Ukraine but also to the West which continued to support Gorbachev's efforts to save the Union. Accordingly, Yeltsin

16 *Komsomolskaya Pravda*, 3 September 1991 (in Brzezinski and Sullivan, 1997: 27).

wrangled with Gorbachev over the nature of the new entity, debating whether it should be a 'democratic confederative state' or a 'confederation of sovereign states', while taking every opportunity to humiliate him in the process (Matlock, 1995; Walker, 2003; Plokhy, 2014).

In parallel, Yeltsin's team maintained dialogue with Ukraine, all the while attempting to derail its drive to independence without formally opposing it. In early November 1991, for example, Russian officials floated the idea of 'Novorossiya', the historical region of the Russian Empire located in south-east Ukraine, as an area of common interest between Russia and Ukraine, a proposal that was firmly rejected by Kyiv (Tarasiuk, 1996). Seeking to maintain constructive relations, Ukraine was eager to reassure Moscow regarding the status of its large Russian minority in Ukraine.[17] On 6 November 1991, the talks produced another communiqué which affirmed the 'unconditional recognition of their [people's] choice as a result of the free expression of their will'. Yet, this was in the context of 'all-round relations of friendship and cooperation, founded upon centuries-old traditions, between the people of Ukraine and Russia', and a desire to keep 'open borders', among other pledges.[18] Thus, the message was inherently contradictory: Moscow would support Ukraine's drive for independence, while maintaining a framework based on the historical unity between Russia and Ukraine.

By the late autumn of 1991, it became clear that the December referendum would result in a vote for independence (Wolczuk,

[17] On 1 November, the Ukrainian Supreme Council passed the Declaration on the Rights of the National Minorities, granting far-reaching collective rights and emphasizing the government's commitment to provide equality to all citizens of Ukraine (Wolczuk, 2001).

[18] https://digitallibrary.un.org/record/132674?ln=en&v=pdf. The communiqué was not the binding commitment Ukraine sought; keen to maximize its symbolic effects, the Ukrainians lodged this document with the UN.

2001). Yeltsin had already refused to sign Gorbachev's draft treaty until Ukraine had done so, despite his repeated insistence that there was no viable alternative to a union. With the results confirmed, Moscow's options narrowed significantly.[19] Yeltsin formally recognized Ukraine's independence and committed to the establishment of new inter-state relations, on the basis of 'the comprehensive and mutually beneficial partnership laid down by the treaty of 19 November 1990 and the communique of 6 November 1991'.[20] The reference to these documents signalled that, in practice, Russia's recognition would not be unconditional.

With Ukraine's leadership now firmly rejecting Gorbachev's plans for a reformed Union, Yeltsin shifted focus to securing a direct deal with Kyiv. The Russian president was ready to compromise with Ukraine as long as, first, the Soviet Union was finally dead, second, the West was satisfied with its orderly dissolution accompanied by a secure transfer of the custody of the nuclear arsenal, and, finally and most importantly, that – even if nominally independent – Ukraine remained united with Russia.

The meeting between the leaders of Russia, Ukraine and Belarus on 7–8 December 1991 achieved two of Yeltsin's key objectives: the formal dissolution of the Soviet Union and the establishment of a unified command over its nuclear arsenal (Plokhy, 2014; Zubok, 2021). The Byelavezha Agreement asserted that the 'USSR has ceased to exist' and placed nuclear weapons under joint control.[21] However, the third objective proved much more problematic. The agreement proclaimed

[19] Zubok (2021: 395) writes that Yeltsin initially asked Bush not to recognize Ukraine immediately, but then suggested that it will recognize it if more than 70 per cent, the majority for Gorbachev's March referendum motion, was exceeded.

[20] 'Yeltsin's post-referendum reaction', *TASS*, 3 December 1991 (in Brzezinski and Sullivan, 1997: 39).

[21] https://digitallibrary.un.org/record/134322?ln=en&v=pdf

the independence of its three signatory states and their status of equal successors of the USSR, a formula that suggested Russia's departure from its imperial past in favour of a new style of relations. Yet, this was insufficient to reassure Kravchuk to enter a new union.

The improvised solution was the creation of the Commonwealth of Independent States (CIS) in place of the USSR: a vaguely defined grouping with no centre, no collective bodies or any other institutional attributes. This left relations among member states to be governed by international agreements. Russia regarded this loose format as distinctly sub-optimal, but remained hopeful: Yeltsin described the CIS as 'the only path towards reintegration of the common post-Soviet space'.[22] Crucially, in line with the 1990 FCA between Russia and Ukraine, Moscow maintained the caveat that borders of the newly independent states are recognized 'within the Commonwealth of Independent States' (Article 5). This phrasing reinforced the conditional nature of Russia's recognition of Ukraine's sovereignty.

Thus, the Byelavezha Agreement averted the immediate collapse of relations. The deal was endorsed by the other former USSR republics on 21 December 1991. However, it soon became apparent in Moscow that 'the Commonwealth does not even exist on paper' (Solchanyk, 1992: 31).

The promise of 'skilful diplomacy'

Russia entered 1992 having formally recognized Ukraine's independence, yet without securing a satisfactory framework for a continued union. The unprecedented and fast-paced changes confronting Yeltsin's team left 'little opportunity for analysis' in the push 'forward into an unknown future' (Kozyrev,

[22] 'Statement before the Russian Parliament', 12 December 1991, https://yeltsin.ru/archive/paperwork/10401.

2019: 71). Nonetheless, amid the uncertainly and disarray, a set of assumptions and imperatives shaped Russia's approach to Ukraine.

To start with, Moscow realized that Ukraine could not be brought back 'into the fold' by force. Yeltsin was determined to distance himself from Gorbachev's legacy, particularly the latter's role in the Baltic crackdowns and his alarmist warnings to Western leaders about a potential Yugoslav-style collapse. Yeltsin positioned himself as the face of a new, non-imperial, post-Soviet Russia, committed to international law. Above all, this image was essential for ensuring the recognition of Russia as the successor state to the USSR. With the US finally abandoning any hope for Gorbachev's reformed union, Washington had premised its support on the OSCE-inspired framework of principles. These included the orderly dissolution of the USSR, respect for existing borders, both 'internal' and external, with any changes occurring peacefully and consensually (Zubok, 2021; Budjeryn, 2023). The strategy proved effective. Thanks to the efforts of British diplomats, the formula of the 'continuation state' was found, enabling all 12 former constituent members of the USSR to be recognized as joint successors of the USSR in law, while designating Russia as the primary heir. Consequently, Russia inherited the principal assets of the USSR, stepped into its international agreements and, crucially, swiftly took over its permanent seat in the UN Security Council (Mullerson, 1993; Zubok, 2021).

The legal terms governing the dissolution of the USSR pointed toward the establishment of 'normal' international relations between the successor states. However, Moscow remained confident that the bonds of history could not be broken, and viewed Ukraine as an unviable state, both politically and economically. The concessions made to Kyiv at Byelavezha were therefore seen as expedient, with Ukraine's independence regarded as a transient phenomenon. As Bukkvoll (2001) observed, Russian communists, nationalists and moderates alike were united by their reluctance to 'normalize' foreign policy with Ukraine, believing that eventual reunification was inevitable.

Unsurprisingly, Moscow focused on strengthening the CIS as the vehicle to a new union, while Ukraine regarded the CIS as merely 'an instrument of consultation, facilitating the resolution of bilateral issues by participating countries' (Tarasiuk, 1996: 13; see Chapter 6). Ironically, however, Ukraine's preference for bilateral inter-state relations provided Russia with ample opportunities to exert varied pressure and assert its control over Ukraine.

As subsequent chapters will demonstrate, Moscow perfected what Burbulis called 'skilful diplomacy' (Zubok, 2021: 364). This marked the beginning of Russia's new, post-Soviet model of dominance in the conditions of Ukraine's nominal independence. On the surface, these interactions represented conventional international relations. Yet, as Evgeniy Ambartsumov, chairman of the Parliamentary International Affairs Committee, put it: 'Totally different methods are needed for the CIS countries. Take negotiations, for example, I do not think they can be as "civilized" as our negotiations with Western countries. … Talks must have more of a "family" atmosphere about them.'[23] Similarly, Dmitri Riurikov, Yeltsin's former adviser, urged Kyiv to make 'a fraternal grand Slavic gesture' and to refrain from constant appeals to its own national laws and international norms in its dealings with Russia (cited in Solchanyk, 1996: 23).

Conclusions

The break-up of the USSR unfolded rapidly and in an improvised manner. Our analysis of Russo-Ukrainian relations in 1990–1 indicates that, despite the nominal recognition of Ukraine's independence, Russia maintained significant

[23] *Rossiyskaya Gazeta*, 13 April 1992 (in Brzezinski and Sullivan, 1997: 90).

caveats. For Moscow, Ukraine's independence was a derivative and temporary state of affairs, with the sword of territorial revision hanging over any Ukrainian actions perceived as a departure from the Russian patrimony. Accordingly, over the next 30 years, Russia developed a new model for bringing Ukraine to heel.

As with the Soviet satellite states, Moscow relied on international law to structure this model. From the Russian perspective, the image of Ukraine's independence and sovereign equality represented a new type of legal fiction to manoeuvre. This approach was facilitated by the West's preoccupation with nuclear control and its sense of relief that the USSR had collapsed without triggering global turmoil.

However, unlike the Warsaw Pact countries, Russia no longer possessed the Communist-era toolbox. In the absence of the glue of the Communist Party, the planned economy and the widespread deployment of troops, the resulting new 'satellite' framework was necessarily looser. So it was to be more discrete and less imposing than the satellite model in Central and Eastern Europe, which had been embedded within the Warsaw Pact and shielded by the Iron Curtain. Nonetheless, the dense and extensive legacies and dependencies stemming from the centralized and integrated nature of the USSR, provided Moscow with ample opportunities to steer Ukraine toward Russia, thanks to the many levers of power Moscow had at its disposal.

Notably, in addition to exploiting Ukraine's extensive dependencies, Russia preyed on Ukraine's strong desire to secure legal guarantees for its independence in the face of the traps already laid down by Russia. Therefore, the post-Soviet 'space' did not evolve into a 'normal' international space, but became a site for the enactment of Russia's patrimonial entitlement in a new legal, institutional and international context.

FOUR

Retaining Russia's Foothold in Ukraine: Crimea and the Black Sea Fleet

As Ukraine sought to consolidate its independence, Moscow's priority from late 1991 was to blunt these efforts. Nowhere was Russian resistance to Ukraine's sovereignty more evident than in the issue of recognizing Ukraine's existing borders and, especially, of Crimea as part of Ukraine's state territory. Although nominally part of the Ukrainian Soviet Socialist Republic since 1954, Crimea held a special historical, ethnic and political significance for Russians, not least due to the presence of the much vaunted Black Sea Fleet (BSF). This was not merely a territorial dispute with Kyiv which the Russian leadership was keen to win; rather, it became a strategic front in Russia's efforts to undermine Ukraine's statehood and assert its patrimonial claims.

We argue that the Crimean question emerged as one of Moscow's primary tools for curtailing Ukraine's statehood in the context of independence. In line with its newly claimed status as an equal, democratic and law-abiding member of the international system, Russia refrained from the forceful border revisions that Yeltsin had initially threatened to prevent Ukraine's secession from the USSR. Moscow repeatedly affirmed its commitment to abide by 'the purposes and principles of the Charter of the United Nations, the Helsinki Final Act and the other documents of the Conference on Security and Cooperation in Europe' (CSCE), which excluded the revision of existing borders in Europe.[1] Nevertheless, Russia challenged Ukraine's statehood in two interconnected ways. First, it supported Crimean separatism, promoting territorial fragmentation. Second, it used the negotiations over the BSF to secure its long-term military presence, thereby maintaining a strategic foothold in Ukraine. This not only undermined Ukraine's pursuit of military independence but also furthered Moscow's ability to intervene in the affairs of Crimea and transform the region into an outpost for its long-term ambitions.

Moscow achieved this by exploiting Ukraine's political and economic vulnerabilities, particularly Kyiv's urgent need for legal recognition for its territorial integrity and borders. In signing the Friendship and Cooperation Treaty in 1997, Russia seemingly recognized Ukraine's sovereignty and inviolability of borders, including Crimea's legal status as part of Ukraine. Yet, as we demonstrate, the deeply unfavourable terms of the Black Sea Fleet Accord, concluded in parallel, revealed that Russia had no intention of accepting an independent Ukraine and relinquishing its control.

Why Crimea?

Crimea's particular role in Russia's power relations with Ukraine rested on a set of overlapping historical, ethnic and strategic narratives (Zaborsky, 1995; Felgenhauer, 1999; Kuzio, 2014, 2020; Darczewska, 2024). Moscow crafted these narratives to single out the Crimean peninsula as a primordial Russian land, thereby establishing it as a powerful lever in realizing its goals for Ukraine.

To begin with, Crimea was unique in being the only region in Ukraine with a majority ethnically Russian population. This

[1] This clause was featured in the bilateral communiqué of 6 November 1991 as well as the Preamble of the Byelavezha Agreement.

demographic feature enabled Moscow to frame Crimea as part of the 'Russian world' and present its policies as a legitimate concern for compatriots abroad. Such framing conveniently obscured Moscow's record of repeated ethnic cleansing and colonization, particularly targeting the indigenous Tatar population (Finnin, 2022).

Following the Russian Empire's conquest of the Crimean Khanate in 1783, sustained violence and discrimination led to mass forced emigration of Tatars to the Ottoman Empire. Under Soviet rule, this trend continued through a combination of ethnic and cultural repression, poverty and starvation. In May 1944, the mass deportations of Tatars to Central Asia – justified by accusations of collaboration with the Nazis – dramatically altered the peninsula's ethnic composition. While Tatars constituted 83 per cent of Crimea's population in 1793, by the late 1980s they had dwindled to just 1.5 per cent (Wilson, 1993: 36). In contrast, the Russian population grew from 5.7 per cent to 67 per cent, a significant number of whom were Soviet BSF personnel and their families. These developments made Crimea a prime example of what has been described as Russia's 'settler colonialism' in the conquered territories (Sumlenny, 2024).

Under Soviet rule, Crimea was initially granted a distinctive political status that could be instrumentalized to serve Russian interests under the guise of self-determination. In 1921, the Bolsheviks created the Crimean Autonomous Soviet Socialist Republic as part of the RSFSR. However, given the totalitarian nature of the Soviet system, this autonomy was largely symbolic and short-lived. Crimea's autonomous status was abolished in June 1945, following the punitive deportation of the Tatars, and was downgraded to an administrative division (*oblast*).[2]

2 While the Crimean Tatars (as well as other nationalities, such as the Volga Germans) were absolved of the charges, they were not allowed to return to their former lands, nor was the autonomous status of Crimea re-established by Moscow (Walker, 2003: 51).

When the self-determination momentum reached Crimea in the late 1980s, calls to restore autonomy drew on historical precedent, offering Russia's elites a new opportunity to exploit the issue.

Famously, in 1954 the peninsula was transferred from the RSFSR to the Ukrainian SSR by a decision of the Presidium of the Supreme Soviet of the USSR. The official reasons for the transfer were, first, the commemoration of the 300th anniversary of the Treaty of Pereyaslav signed between the Cossack Hetmanate and the Tsardom of Russia, and, second, the natural outgrowth of 'the territorial proximity of Crimea to Ukraine, the commonalities of their economies, and the close agricultural and cultural ties between the Crimean oblast and the UkrSSR' (Kramer, 2014). While the former reinforced the myth of Russian-Ukrainian unity, the latter reflected pragmatic concerns arising from the Soviet mismanagement of Crimea. Yet, as Kramer (2014) argues, the justification for this decision was complex, including a desire to fortify Soviet control over Ukraine by increasing its Russian population. In Russia, the 1954 transfer came to be viewed as the whim of the Soviet leaders and an act of historical injustice, which reinforced the view of Ukraine as an artificial state constructed during Soviet times.

Finally, a special place in Russia's historical narrative was reserved for Sevastopol, the city founded by Catherine the Great as Russia's Black Sea naval base soon after the conquest of Crimea. Sevastopol became emblematic as 'the city of Russian glory', an image rooted in the imperial myths of the heroism of the Russian people in the Crimean War (1853–6) (Plokhy, 2000). This image was revived in the Soviet era and reinforced by the glorification of the heroic battles of the Second World War. Sevastopol was further distinguished in 1948 when it was granted the special status of a closed city as the base of the Soviet BSF. With restricted access and direct administration from Moscow, Sevastopol became a Soviet stronghold within Ukraine.

The spectre of separatism

By the end of the 1990s, calls to restore Crimean autonomy mirrored the broader awakening of national identities in the late Soviet Union. In an effort to pre-empt nationalist-separatist pressures, the Ukrainian parliament voted in February 1991 to establish the Crimean Autonomous Republic (Kuzio, 2014). Importantly, this step was also interpreted as an expression of pluralism, inclusiveness and historical justice.

Following Ukraine's declaration of independence, Crimea participated in the referendum of 1 December 1991, with 54 per cent of voters supporting independence, including 57 per cent in Sevastopol.[3] Nonetheless, pro-Russian forces and senior Russian politicians openly advocated for Crimea to rejoin Russia. Emboldened by Russia's assertive efforts to take over the Soviet BSF (discussed later), and spurred by Vice President Alexander Rutskoy's provocative interventions in early April, the Crimean parliament voted on 5 May 1992 to declare independence, to be confirmed in a later referendum. It also adopted a constitution, proclaiming the 'Republic of Crimea' as a 'sovereign state'. As with similar declarations at the time, the legal meaning of this proclamation of 'sovereignty' was ambiguous (Walker, 2003). This constitution described Crimea as part of the Ukrainian state, yet simultaneously asserted that relations between 'sovereign' Crimea and Ukraine should be based on treaties and agreements (Tatarenko, 2014). Kyiv rejected the declaration of independence as invalid. By offering greater autonomy and a special economic status, it negotiated a resolution that reaffirmed Crimea's position as an autonomous republic and, critically, as an integral part of Ukraine. This was reflected in the September 1992 amendments to the Crimean Constitution.

3 Ukraine's leader, Leonid Kravchuk, successfully persuaded the Crimean authorities not to hold a separate referendum on independence from Ukraine (Plokhy, 2015).

In 1993, Ukraine's worsening economic situation provided renewed justification for separatism. The Crimean parliament passed several measures to strengthen Crimean autonomy and created the office of the President of Crimea. In January 1994, Yuri Meshkov was elected president in a campaign managed by covert operatives from Moscow (Zaborsky, 1995). Promoting union with Russia, Meshkov introduced a series of initiatives, including a return to the May 1992 Crimean Constitution and a proposed referendum on Crimea's independence from Ukraine. However, throughout 1994, Kyiv engaged in dialogue with the Crimean leaders and ultimately succeeded in diffusing the separatist momentum. This was formalized through a sequence of constitutional measures, including the abolition of the Crimean presidency, the adoption of a new Crimean Constitution and the comprehensive definition of the scope of Crimea's autonomy in Ukraine's 1996 Constitution (Wolczuk, 2001).[4]

Yeltsin's restraint on Crimean separatism is particularly noteworthy. By 1994, he had become acutely aware of the risks of setting a precedent for Russia's own constituent autonomous republics and regions, especially in light of Chechnya's push for independence. In response to Kyiv's assertive actions to uphold Ukraine's jurisdiction, Yeltsin declared the Crimean issue to be an internal matter for Ukraine, despite contrary statements from senior Russian politicians (Zaborsky, 1995). Once Moscow launched its military campaign in Chechnya in late 1994, the overt promotion of the territorial revisionism in Ukraine subsided.

Importantly, Russia did not withdraw from interfering in Crimean politics. On the contrary, Moscow remained deeply

[4] While Ukraine's elites rejected a federal model for Ukraine at large, the view was that extensive autonomy was indispensable to placate the centrifugal forces and prevent separatism in Crimea. Therefore, Crimea was the only region of Ukraine that was granted territorial autonomy in an otherwise unitary state (Wolczuk, 2001).

engaged in supporting and funding pro-Russian groups and politicians (Lutsevych, 2016). Yet, its primary focus shifted to securing the best deal on the BSF, which came to be viewed as the Russian military and political foothold in Crimea and a platform for boosting control over all of Ukraine.

The BSF and Crimea: exploring the options

For Russia, one of the most troubling aspects of Ukraine's drive for independence was Kyiv's push to create its own military forces by claiming authority over Soviet forces and facilities located on Ukrainian territory.[5] Ukraine's efforts to subordinate all military assets within its borders to the Ukraine parliament symbolized not only Russia's loss of the BSF but also the perception that Kyiv was on course to 'completely sever the special relations with Russia, including [in] the military and political sphere' (Budjeryn, 2023: 141). Several legal and political options were employed to prevent such an outcome. This intense contestation between Russia and Ukraine was emblematic of Russia's sense of entitlement over Ukraine and its attempt to hollow out Ukraine's formal sovereignty, but without overtly denying it.

Initially, Russia hoped that the creation of the CIS as a common military-strategic space would secure its control over the BSF and its Crimean base under the umbrella of CIS joint command.[6] However, Ukraine's rejection of the concept of joined armed forces, undermined this strategy. Viewing military independence as essential to asserting its statehood, Kyiv was adamant that 'everything stationed or deployed on

5 This approach was in contrast to the one taken by the Baltic countries which demanded the withdrawal of all Soviet forces and, following which, built their national armies from scratch (Budjeryn, 2023).

6 The Byelavezha Agreement envisaged 'a common military-strategic space, including unified control over nuclear weapons', a clause essential to satisfy international concerns about the fate of the Soviet nuclear arsenal.

[Ukraine's] territory must belong to Ukraine' (Felgenhauer, 1999: 7). In contrast to Moscow, Kyiv interpreted the CIS common space as applying solely to nuclear assets and facilities, in line with its commitment to denuclearization (Budjeryn, 2023).[7] Accordingly, Kyiv excluded the BSF from CIS strategic command, except for vessels carrying nuclear weapons.[8]

In response to Kyiv's defiance, Moscow again raised the threat of territorial revision. In January 1992, Vladimir Lukin, a prominent parliamentarian and close ally of Yeltsin, proposed that Russia claim the entire BSF and re-examine the legality of the 1954 transfer of Crimea as the best lever to compel Kyiv to accept Russia's plans.[9] Acting on this suggestion, on 21 May 1992 the Russian parliament declared the decision on the 1954 transfer of Crimea to Ukraine 'null and void from the moment of its adoption'. While the declaration appeared to respect Russia's commitments under the CSCE, it simultaneously called for negotiations with Ukraine on Crimea's future status. Ukraine vehemently rejected such requests, exposing the legal rationale behind the claim of illegality as false, politically motivated and in violation of Russia's international

7 Moscow endorsed the plans of Yevgeny Shaposhnikov, the head of the Soviet Ministry of Defence, to transform the USSR force into a comprehensive CIS armed force under a single command (Brzezinski and Sullivan, 1997: 444). In line with this approach, the CIS Agreement on the Strategic Forces, concluded on 30 December 1991, referred to CIS joint command over military units and installations with nuclear weapons as well as 'other units agreed by the member states', a precise list of which was to be compiled later.

8 A protocol of a working group meeting of 16 January 1992 listed the BSF as part of the strategic forces, with Ukrainian President Kravchuk's hand-written caveat 'except for the parts of the BSF that will form part of the Armed Forces of Ukraine' (Eberle, 1992: 159). At the same time, Ukraine's Defence Minister Morozov was tasked with determining which vessels should be transferred to CIS command.

9 Lukin's proposal also referred to various forms of economic pressure (Budjeryn, 2023: 141).

obligations.[10] Kyiv also sought to bolster its position by reconsidering its denuclearization stance, eventually making it conditional on receiving explicit security guarantees from Russia and the international community (Budjeryn, 2023).

The Russian parliament, however, escalated its legal challenge in July 1992 by focusing on the status of Sevastopol. It argued that the city had not been part of the 1954 transfer of Crimea due to its special designation, which placed it outside Ukraine's jurisdiction. Ultimately, in July 1993, the Supreme Soviet took unilateral action, decreeing Sevastopol to have Russian federal status. Ukraine protested the move before the UN Security Council, denouncing it as a 'flagrant flouting' of the fundamental principles and norms of international law, securing its condemnation.[11]

Yeltsin was keen to distance himself from these claims, even though his own view was that 'the Black Sea Fleet has been, is still, and will remain Russian' (Galeotti, 1994: 51). He acted on Lukin's proposal by claiming exclusive control over the BSF on 7 April 1992, following Kyiv's similar declaration two days earlier. Nevertheless, Yeltsin pursued a gradual diplomatic resolution.[12] Peaceful settlement was essential not only to affirm Russia's international credentials, but also to secure Ukraine's cooperation on key issues, including the future of the CIS and the completion of Russia's take-over of the Soviet nuclear arsenal (Budjeryn, 2023). Accordingly, Yeltsin's team

[10] Declaration of the Supreme Rada of Ukraine of 2 June 1992, https://digitallibrary.un.org/record/144725/files/A_47_260-EN.pdf.

[11] Decision of 20 July 1993: Statement by the President of the UN Security Council, https://main.un.org/securitycouncil/sites/default/files/en/sc/repertoire/93-95/Chapter%208/EUROPE/93-95_8-22-UKRAINE.pdf.

[12] In advance of the Byelavezha meeting, Yeltsin was advised to push Kravchuk to agree on border revision after a moratorium of 3–5 years (Zubok, 2021: 401). In the rush to secure a deal, Yeltsin did not raise this at Byelavezha. Yet in effect this is what Yeltsin pushed for in the talks with Kravchuk in the summer of 1992.

condemned the July 1993 Decree on Sevastopol, asserting that it diverged from official policy 'as regards matters relating to the Black Sea fleet and in maintaining bases for the navy of the Russian Federation in Ukraine, in the Crimea and in Sevastopol' and that such matters could be 'settled only through political dialogue, taking into consideration the opinions and interests of the various population groups'.[13]

For Moscow, the notion of a 'negotiated solution' entailed the use of political and economic instruments which, in practice, left Ukraine with little choice but to comply. This approach was facilitated by Ukraine's economic vulnerabilities, particularly its heavy dependence on Russian energy. At the heart of Russia's strategy, however, was the substitution of overt territorial revisionism with the instrumentalization of legal uncertainty. This opportunity presented itself owing to Kyiv's desire to secure a binding commitment from Russia to respect Ukraine's territorial integrity. Yeltsin could capitalize on the ambiguities embedded in the existing bilateral agreements, especially the qualified recognition of the inviolability of Ukraine's existing borders 'within the USSR'[14] (as stated in the 1990 bilateral FCA with Ukraine) or 'within the Commonwealth' (as per the Byelavezha Agreement).[15] According to Yuri Dubinin, deputy foreign minister and a member of Russia's negotiating team, the plan was to condition the preparation of a general *political* treaty, one that would include the legal guarantees sought by Ukraine, on the negotiations over the BSF: 'Then Russia

[13] Decision of 20 July 1993: Statement by the President of the UN Security Council.

[14] Ironically, despite the clause Moscow chose to centre on, for Ukraine this accord provided the only binding commitment Russia had made to its territorial integrity at all, and Kyiv was therefore keen to invoke it too.

[15] Article 5 of the Byelavezha Agreement bound its signatories to 'acknowledge and respect each other's territorial integrity and the inviolability of existing borders within the Commonwealth'.

would possess the diplomatic resource to find a solution to the Black Sea Fleet problem' (Dubinin, 2007: 4–5).

Thus, the promise of a bilateral political agreement became a strategic trap into which Moscow sought to lure Kyiv. In doing so, Moscow appeared to honour its broad international commitments, making seemingly significant concessions. For example, Yeltsin eventually dropped the caveat that Russia's recognition of Ukraine's territorial integrity applied only 'within the CIS'. This commitment was reflected in the Trilateral Statement between Russia, Ukraine and the US of January 1994 and the Budapest Memorandum of September 1994, both of which affirmed the CSCE principle that border changes must occur only through peaceful and consensual means (Budjeryn, 2023).

In reality, these lofty proclamations masked an ongoing battle over the BSF, which persisted even after the election of the pro-Russian President Leonid Kuchma in July 1994. When it became clear that Kuchma was unwilling to concede to Moscow's demands on the BSF base, negotiations stalled. Every milestone in the legal process toward a treaty was used to exert pressure on Ukraine, beginning with the mere promise of a future agreement. Even after the draft was initialled in early 1995, Yeltsin withheld final signature, objecting to Ukraine's efforts to decouple the BSF issue from that of the general political treaty in order to 'outwit Russia' (Dubinin, 2007: 10). Russia proved to be a difficult negotiating partner, frequently reneging on commitments when Ukraine's economic position weakened or when circumstances allowed it, as illustrated in the chronological timeline in Table 4.1, which will be explored in more detail in the next section.

Aware of Russia's agenda, Ukraine pursued a dual-track strategy, seeking closer ties with the West. Moscow, intent on 'gatekeeping' its patrimony, grew increasingly concerned about Ukraine's engagement with Western institutions. Ukraine's warming relationship ties with NATO were particularly troubling for Moscow and ultimately forced its hand. The

Table 4.1: Legal milestones in the division of the BSF

Agreements	Key terms
Dagomys, 23 June 1992	To negotiate the creation of two navies in place of the USSR BSF. Until then, maintain existing arrangements on CIS joint command, with parties refraining from unilateral action.
Yalta, 3 August 1992	To divide the BSF, following a transition period until 1995, with details subject to a separate agreement. Agreed joint use and joint command of the fleet under the presidents of Russia and Ukraine. Agreement on further arrangements to follow.
Moscow, 17 June 1993	To accelerate efforts and begin division on a 50:50 basis from September 1993. An inter-state commission to be set up to this effect. Rules on interim joint command and financing arrangements agreed. The terms of Russia's basing to be agreed later. Russia has the right to participate in the economic and social development of Sevastopol and other cities where its troops and infrastructure are based.
Massandra, 3 September 1993	The whole of the fleet and all its infrastructure in Crimea will pass to Russia in exchange for a payment equal to Ukraine's gas debt.
Moscow, 15 April 1994	Ukraine to receive 15–20% of the vessels. The details of this division to be arranged in a further agreement. The two fleets will be based separately.
Sochi, 9 June 1995	Ukraine will receive 18.3% of the vessels, with compensation for the remaining 31.7% of its share. The two fleets will be based separately. Sevastopol will be 'the main base' of the Russian Federation. The Russian BSF will 'use' the base infrastructure. Russia has the right to participate in the socio-economic development of Sevastopol and its other bases. The terms of Russia's stay on Ukraine's territory will be subject to another agreement.
Kyiv, 31 May 1997	Agreed list of vessels and equipment as the property of each party.

(continued)

Table 4.1: Legal milestones in the division of the BSF (continued)

Agreements	Key terms
	Agreed compensation that Ukraine will receive for the remainder of its share. Sevastopol will be 'the main base' of the Russian BSF. Russia will use several listed berths. Agreed status and parameters of Russia's stay, including a 20-year term, extendable by five years.
Kharkiv, 21 April 2010	Term extended by additional 25 years (until 2042) with an option of a further five-year renewal (until 2047).

planned signing of a NATO–Ukraine Charter at the July 1997 Madrid summit compelled Yeltsin to finally sign the Friendship Treaty in May 1997 – though not before concluding the deal on the BSF just days earlier.[16]

The Friendship Treaty appeared to mark a major milestone in Russia–Ukraine relations. For many observers, it represented the long-awaited unequivocal formal recognition of Ukraine's sovereignty and inviolability of 'existing borders'. As Larrabee argued, the treaty 'ended the cat and mouse game that Moscow had played since 1991', thereby, removing 'Crimea and Sevastopol as points of contention in Russian-Ukraine relations' (1996: 253). It seemed that it 'closed the questions of Ukraine's sovereignty and territorial integrity' in line with the norms of universal international law (D'Anieri, 2012: 449).

16 The game of using the lever of the general treaty to get the BSF deal continued even after signing the accords. The Ukraine Rada ratified the Friendship Treaty but was not keen to sign off on the BSF agreements. Concerned about the loss of its key leverage to secure its military presence, the Russian Federation Council conditioned its own ratification of the Friendship Treaty on Ukraine's ratification of the BSF accords, ultimately delaying the process until the middle of 1999 (Dubinin, 2007).

However, such assessments proved overly optimistic. The BSF deal, which was a prerequisite to the treaty's signing, was deeply unfavourable to Ukraine on multiple levels, casting doubt on the treaty's actual significance. Indeed, in 2014, the commitments Russia had made in the 1997 Friendship Treaty were comprehensively violated, while the BSF and the control over Sevastopol played a pivotal role in the dismemberment of Ukraine.

Unpacking the BSF deal

The BSF deal merits close re-examination. Dividing the BSF required not only an agreement on the allocation of vessels and equipment between two fleets, but also, crucially, on the basing arrangements and the legal status of Sevastopol and the rest of Crimea. While the final agreement formally affirmed Ukraine's legal sovereignty over Crimea, its military and economic terms were not to Ukraine's advantage (Sherr, 1997). Three key aspects of the negotiations illustrate how Russia's control was perpetuated, as outlined in the following brief review of the dynamic of the talks and their outcomes.

First, even though most BSF vessels were outdated and in poor condition, Moscow was determined to secure the bulk of the fleet. A large fleet was not only symbolically important but also justified extensive basing needs, thereby enabling a larger Russian presence. Moscow's initial proposal for an 80:20 split was rejected by Ukraine.[17] Amid the stalemate, Yeltsin proposed at Yalta in August 1992 to postpone the talks until 1995. In the interim, the fleet was to be removed from CIS control and placed under a joint Russia–Ukraine command.

[17] One of Kyiv's objections was that having accepted a 16.7 per cent share of the external debt of the USSR, they were entitled to the same percentage of its assets, which was well above the value of the *entire* BSF as a percentage of the total former Soviet Fleet (Eberle, 1992). Therefore, Kyiv also rejected the reduced 60:40 offer.

While the formula served Moscow's interests, Ukraine soon protested Russia's unilateral redeployment of military hardware and its distortion of the Yalta agreement (Felgenhauer, 1999). In July 1993, under pressure from threats of oil price hikes and gas supply cuts, Ukraine agreed to a 50:50 split with Russia leasing its base from Ukraine, though on terms to be agreed in a subsequent agreement (Hill and Jewett, 1994). However, just months later at Massandra, capitalizing on Ukraine's mounting economic difficulties, Yeltsin reversed course and pressured Kravchuk to transfer Ukraine's share of the fleet to Russia in exchange for a reduction in gas debt.

Under President Kuchma, negotiations resumed and a division was agreed in June 1995, though its financial terms remained highly contentious. The final 1997 agreement closely resembled Russia's opening position: Ukraine received only 18.7 per cent of the fleet. For the 31.3 per cent ceded to Russia, Ukraine was compensated with a $521 million reduction in its energy debt, far below Ukraine's demands and its valuation of the fleet.[18]

Second, despite Ukraine's efforts, Russia emerged from the negotiations with de facto control over Sevastopol. Kyiv successfully resisted Russian demands to lease the entire city rather than the naval base.[19] Moscow had insisted that the fleet's maintenance and servicing required authority over the whole of the city's infrastructure (Zaborsky, 1995; Sherr, 1997). However, Moscow ultimately secured near exclusive control over the Sevastopol base by rejecting Kyiv's demands for joint basing.[20] This outcome was facilitated by the drawn-out and

[18] This indicates a total valuation of the fleet at some $1.6 billion, rather than the $80 billion Kyiv originally claimed the fleet was worth.

[19] The Ukrainians were unsuccessful in persuading Moscow to move out of Sevastopol and be stationed at other naval bases in Crimea.

[20] Moscow argued that Ukraine did not need access to such a big naval base and that sharing the base would complicate the command of both fleets (Zaborsky, 1995). As Sherr (1997) notes, there was also the fear

piecemeal nature of the negotiations. Ukraine's position was weakened already in 1995, when the Sochi Accord designated Sevastopol as Russia's 'main base', while the location of Ukraine's 'main base' remained undecided. Yeltsin attempted to formalize this in April 1996 by insisting Sevastopol's formal designation as an 'exclusive' base (Sherr, 1997). Although the final agreement nominally referred to 'joint' basing, in practice Moscow secured exclusive rights to Sevastopol's main bays. The Ukrainian navy was left with inferior berthing facilities in both quantity and quality. Ukraine's legal victories, thus, proved largely symbolic. Meanwhile, Moscow secured a broad clause granting it the right to participate in the economic and social development of Sevastopol and Crimean cities hosting its troops and infrastructure.

Third, the legitimation of Russia's military presence in Crimea was widely perceived in Ukraine as a significant blow to the country's sovereignty. Domestic opposition was strong, evident during the drafting of Ukraine's new constitution (Wolczuk, 2001). Under Russian pressure, on 28 June 1996 President Kuchma pushed through a special transitional clause: while the constitution forbade foreign military bases on Ukraine's territory, this clause allowed for 'the use of existing military bases on the territory of Ukraine for the temporary stationing of foreign military formations … on the terms of lease'.[21] The lease granted Russia the right to maintain forces on Ukrainian soil for 20–25 years. Although this was less than Moscow's initial demand, it was a far cry from Ukraine's original hope that any lease would be a short-term arrangement to facilitate Russia's withdrawal from the territory of Ukraine

that joint basing might result in Kyiv leasing Crimean facilities to NATO at some point in the future.

21 Article 17 of the 1996 Constitution provided that 'foreign military bases shall not be permitted on the territory of Ukraine'. In effect, the transitional clause was to Moscow's long-term advantage as it kept Russia in, but any other 'foreign' force out.

and the relocation of the fleet's headquarters, potentially to Novorossiysk. Ukraine was soon to discover that Russia had no intention of leaving Crimea.

Extending Russian control

Once locked into the BSF agreements, Ukraine found itself with limited options to reverse its fortunes. In 2009, amid heightened concerns following the 2008 Russia–Georgia war, the then President Yushchenko announced that Ukraine would not extend the BSF lease beyond its 20-year term ending in 2017 (D'Anieri, 2019). In response, President Medvedev accused Kyiv of violating the 1997 BSF Agreements, issuing a strongly worded reprimand to the Ukrainian leadership.[22] In a foretaste of future developments, Medvedev's address invoked the historical unity of the Russian and Ukrainian peoples, accusing Kyiv of betraying it for 'short-term considerations'. Then, in October 2009, the Kremlin introduced a bill authorizing the deployment of troops abroad to defend Russians and 'prevent aggression', a move interpreted as a prelude to the eventual military seizure of Crimea (Rumer and Kramer, 2009).

The issue appeared to dissipate in early 2010 when the election of pro-Russian President Viktor Yanukovych ended what Moscow described as the five-year 'black streak' (*chernoi polosy*) in Russia–Ukraine relations.[23] Russia quickly moved to consolidate its hold on Crimea. In April 2010, Yanukovych and Medvedev signed the Kharkiv Accords, which extended the BSF lease to 2042 in exchange for a discount on the existing gas pricing formula. This was a secretive and non-transparent deal, designed to minimize domestic opposition in Ukraine.

[22] Address to the President of Ukraine Victor Yushchenko, 13 August 2009, http://en.kremlin.ru/supplement/4938.

[23] '*Rossisko-ukrainskie peregovory na vysshem urovne*', 5 March 2020, http://kremlin.ru/events/president/news/7041.

As Sherr (2010) notes, the arrangement extended Russia's rights without addressing any of the deficiencies of the 1997 BSF deal. Its detrimental impact was compounded by the fact that the gas discount was structured as a debt offset, failing to reduce prices in real terms and entrenching Ukraine's energy dependence on Russia.[24] In effect, the Kharkiv deal, linking the BSF base to energy pricing, served only to further weaken Ukraine's hand.

Conclusions

Ukraine's desire to preserve its territorial integrity and eliminate the presence of foreign troops from its soil reflected a deep-seated anxiety about Russia's persistent reluctance to accept an independent Ukrainian state (Wolczuk, 2002). For Russia, the 'loss' of Crimea symbolized a reduction in its patrimony and diminution of its status as regional hegemon. At the same time, Ukraine's eagerness for legal assurances presented Moscow with an opportunity. On the one hand, Russia could demonstrate to the international community that it was a responsible actor committed to international norms. On the other hand, it retained a suite of levers to halt the erosion of its reach and potentially reverse it over time. Ukraine's urgent need for recognition of its sovereignty and territorial integrity, for which it was clearly prepared to pay a high price, became a focal point for Russia's efforts.

While stoking separatism proved problematic, Russia's tactic of using the division of the BSF to establish a new basis for its patrimonial hold on Crimea was highly effective. Despite formal designations, Russia retained near-total control over the fleet and its Sevastopol base at minimal financial cost. It preserved its military preponderance in the Black Sea, as

[24] Only days after the accord, Russia sought to acquire de facto control over the jewel in Ukraine's crown – its energy infrastructure.

demonstrated by the use of BSF assets in regional conflicts, notably against Georgia in 2008. In the longer term, Russia secured the legitimate presence of its forces on Ukrainian territory – forces which could be, and ultimately were, deployed against Ukraine and other littoral states, with no legal recourse available to prevent such actions.

For Ukraine, there was no viable alternative to seeking legal guarantees, particularly as its efforts to secure robust international support and security assurances proved largely futile. Kyiv negotiated from a position of political, economic and military weakness, a reality reflected in the agreements it signed. They legitimized the presence of Russian forces on Ukrainian soil, while the debt and gas price reductions proved illusory. Ukraine relinquished significant military assets and agreed to host forces that, when the moment came, were used to attack it by land and by sea. Although Kyiv ostensibly achieved its primary objective – the formal recognition of its sovereignty and territorial integrity by Russia – even this success proved hollow. Russia's recognition remained conditional upon Ukraine's continued deference to Moscow's claims.

FIVE

Playing with Borders

For Ukraine, formalizing its state borders with all its neighbours, but above all with Russia, was an overwhelming priority. This was not merely the typical concern of a newly independent state seeking defined territory and borders as integral components of its sovereign statehood. Kyiv's urgency to secure Ukraine's borders stemmed from the historical discontinuities and the instrumental approach to border definition that had long characterized Eastern Europe.[1] As part of the USSR, the Ukrainian SSR had official republican territory and borders. Yet, the borders were largely nominal and unmarked, with their status ultimately determined in Moscow. The issue was not just technical; it was about containing patrimonial sentiments in Moscow, which continued to cast doubt on Ukraine's 'existing borders', as discussed in the previous chapter. Ukrainian leaders believed that enshrining borders in the articles of a formal treaty would offer at least some form of defence against the perceived threat from Russia.

Border definition is a complex process, both practically and politically (OSCE, 2017). First, borders must be *delimited*, that is agreed and legally defined by being plotted on maps and described topographically in bilateral treaties. Second, they must be *demarcated*, that is physically marked on the ground. Even among the best of neighbours, the technical challenges

1 Ukraine's Rada passed a new Law on the State Borders on 4 November 1991, even before the independence referendum had taken place.

of agreeing on and establishing a 1,974-km inter-state land border and a 321-km maritime border would be considerable. However, Russia's sheer recalcitrance in cooperating and committing to respecting Ukraine's territorial integrity vastly exacerbated these difficulties. For Moscow, the establishment of real state borders was the most visible sign of the partition of its patrimony. Fully fledged state borders threatened to make permanent what was viewed as a temporary indulgence of Ukraine's independence. They symbolized Ukraine's statehood, but also clashed with Russia's patrimonial tradition and the 'psychological map of its borders', which exceeded the boundaries of the Russian Federation (Kuzio, 1997: 38).

This chapter demonstrates Moscow's complex manoeuvring around borders. While it formally adhered to the international etiquette of recognizing Ukraine's independence, its deep reluctance to agree on border definition with Ukraine betrayed more sinister motives. It was the primary expression of Russia's entitlement over Ukraine: as Konstantin Zatulin, chair of the Duma CIS Committee, bluntly stated, there was no need to recognize the 'historically non-existent borders of a historically non-existent state' (cited in Solchanyk, 1996: 30).

Given the inherently bilateral nature of border definition, Ukraine's eagerness to settle the issue provided Russia with valuable leverage. Some regarded the conclusion of Russia–Ukraine agreements, such as the 2003 State Border Agreement and the 2003 Azov Sea and Kerch Strait Agreement, as proof that Russia had settled the matter and recognized Ukraine's existence (Sakwa, 2019). However, Moscow's apparent earnestness was largely performative. The close analysis of these agreements reveals a more complex picture: they provided a veneer of legality but did little to alter the border status quo inherited from the Soviet Union. Land borders were defined on paper, but progress in demarcation was limited and subordinated to Moscow's broader goal of drawing Ukraine back into a union. In the maritime domain, Russia conceded even less: not only did it refuse delimitation, but it furthered its own freedom of action in the Azov Sea and the Kerch Strait, thereby consolidating its hegemony in the region. In the process, the Kremlin expanded its toolkit. As early as 2003, it attempted territorial revisions by seeking to incorporate the island of Tuzla in the Kerch Strait. Overall, the border agreements fuelled uncertainty around Ukraine's statehood and constrained Kyiv's ability to defend itself against future Russian encroachments.

Land borders

In the USSR, internal borders nominally delineated the territories of the union republics. Yet they made little difference due to the centralized nature of the state. Inter-republican borders served only administrative purposes: there was no border infrastructure, no border guards, nor custom officials. Whatever delineation existed, it was imprecise, based on large-scale historical maps. In addition, the frequent shifts in territory between the republics, a notorious practice by Moscow, were rarely documented properly (Musafirova, 2023). The various holdings and infrastructure that had been built up over the decades and which spanned the border areas, further compounded the challenge. Thus, defining those borders in a precise way was going to be an arduous task even among the most willing of partners. Yet, the technical difficulty was overshadowed by Russia's opposition to the process as it would amount to the ultimate recognition of Ukraine's independence.

Russia's initial approach was to seek to preserve the status quo through the principle of 'open borders', reflected in its initial dealings with independent Ukraine – both bilaterally and within the framework of the CIS (see Chapter 3).[2] To this end, Moscow insisted that the internal borders of

[2] For example, the communiqué of 6 November 1991, Article 5 of the Byelavezha Agreement, the 23 June 1992 Dagomys Agreement.

the newly established grouping should remain porous and transparent. From the Russian perspective, official acts of border definition were deemed unnecessary between the former Soviet republics in order to ensure the free movement of people. Indeed, Russia's political elites consistently insisted that no borders between 'fraternal peoples' should exist (Kuzio, 1997). However, Moscow acted unilaterally when it suited its interests. Hence, the Kremlin was equally keen to introduce customs controls in late 1992. This served Russia's economic priorities, while also providing Moscow with a new lever in dealing with its neighbours.[3]

Even when the CIS project stalled, Russia did not alter its position on borders, indicating a continued lack of interest in a bilateral agreement on border delineation. Moscow consistently eschewed Ukraine's calls to commence the process,[4] expressing no more than 'intent to negotiate' when politically expedient. For example, Moscow made symbolic gestures at key points in the talks on the BSF, thereby boosting Moscow's leverage (see Chapter 4).[5]

The tactics of blocking border definition became harder to justify following the conclusion of the 1997 Friendship Treaty, which signalled Russia's apparently unconditional recognition of Ukraine's statehood and borders. Yet, even though formal talks on delineation finally began in 1998, Russia's underlying sentiment remained unchanged. The need for borders between

3 Russia proceeded to set up a series of hub-and-spoke free trade agreements, which allowed for numerous exemptions on 'sensitive' goods, the imposition of arbitrary trade protection measures and customs controls, which it increasingly began to deploy to achieve non-economic objectives (Dragneva and de Kort, 2007).

4 The Ukrainian authorities submitted nearly twenty diplomatic notes requesting the start of negotiations prior to 1997 (Kuzio, 1997: 40).

5 For example, a protocol of intent on the demarcation of borders between Ukraine and Russia was signed in December 1995 and an agreement was reached on the necessity of starting the legal delimitation of borders In September 1996.

'the people of one nation' continued to be opposed. Russia's representatives continued to invoke the 1990 bilateral FCA with its clause on respecting territorial integrity only within the USSR as a means of countering Ukrainian demands for progress (Musafirova, 2023). The 1997 treaty did not overcome Russia's fundamental objection to the consolidation of Ukraine's statehood.

Notably, Russia's cooperation picked up pace only when it wanted to attract Ukraine to a Russia-led regional project (see Chapter 6). The unblocking of border delineation in 2002 formed part of Putin's charm offensive, aimed at enticing Ukraine's embattled president, Leonid Kuchma, to commit to the Eurasian Economic Community and its successor project in 2003, the Common Economic Space.[6] Thus, the Kremlin signed the Treaty on the Russia–Ukraine State Border in January 2003, an act consistent with Moscow's revised tactic of avoiding open challenges to Ukraine's independence and emphasizing Ukraine's status as an 'equal brother and friend' (Kupchinski, 2003). The treaty was significant as it offered Ukraine the formal delimitation of the land borders Kyiv had long sought. Yet, the Ukrainian side was justifiably sceptical about the credibility of Moscow's legal undertakings. Indeed, the treaty was widely understood as an act of political symbolism, little more than a ceremonial gesture to accompany the launch of the declared 'Year of Ukraine in Russia' (Zhurzhenko, 2007). Unsurprisingly, Ukraine's negotiators sought enhanced guarantees by pushing for a clause stipulating that the treaty could not be denounced, a provision Russia rejected (Musafirova, 2023).

More importantly, the Ukrainians were keen to secure the stability of the newly delineated borders by seeking to make

6 In 2002–03, Kuchma was isolated internationally and losing political support domestically following his implication in the murder of Georgy Gongadze, a journalist critical of the regime.

them visible on the ground and thus pushing for demarcation, beginning with the establishment of a demarcation commission. Kyiv argued that 'demarcated borders are legally indispensable between sovereign countries' (Jamestown Foundation, 2002). Furthermore, demarcation was increasingly seen as essential to Ukraine's ability to implement effective anti-terrorism and anti-smuggling border regimes, and thus to enable its developing cooperation with the EU and NATO (Zhurzhenko, 2007).

Moscow was prepared to update and make a more precise topographical record of the borders on maps but had no intention of demarcating them on the ground. As Russia's envoy, the Deputy Foreign Minister Loshchinin put it, such a step would 'go against the grain of "traditional" Russian-Ukrainian relations, and would interfere with economic, cultural and human contacts between the two countries, their border regions and their residents'; he also chided the Ukrainians about being 'hotheads' in making such demands (cited in Jamestown Foundation, 2002). Moscow's opposition to border demarcation was increasingly viewed as a tactic to stall Ukraine's deepening cooperation with the EU and NATO, while framing Kyiv's demands as externally driven rather than the choice of the Ukrainians.[7]

Unsurprisingly, the promise of 'progressing toward' demarcation remained central to Moscow's dealings with Ukraine. For example, in 2010, this promise formed part of an elaborate package of incentives aimed at persuading the newly elected President Yanukovych to extend the BSF lease in Crimea and join Russia's latest integration initiative, the Eurasian Customs Union. Tellingly, the agreement on the demarcation of land borders signed in May 2010 was a brief document, which – yet again – provided little detail beyond

[7] See, for example, Viktor Chernomyrdin cited in 'Russian ambassador says Ukraine, Russia "not ready" for border demarcation', RFERL Newsline, 30 April 2002, https://www.rferl.org/a/1142666.html.

the familiar 'signalling the intent' to launch demarcation and to appoint a bilateral commission to carry it out.

Ukraine's closer ties with the EU, however, prompted Russia to signal readiness for concessions. The fact that, after 20 years of stalling, demarcation work finally commenced is best explained by Russia's determination to win Kyiv's commitment in the face of the progress toward Ukraine's Association Agreement with the EU, which despite the complications, was inching toward completion (Dragneva and Wolczuk, 2015a). Thus, finally, on 7 November 2012, the first border post was placed ceremonially at the 'Three Sisters' border crossing between Russia, Belarus and Ukraine, an unsubtle reference to historic Slavic unity. Nonetheless, the subsequent progress remained very limited, with demarcation plans extending only to the Sumy and Chernihiv regions (two out of five border regions).

Within 18 months, Russia's cooperation ended completely as part of its offensive against Ukraine's new government in early 2014 (see Chapter 7). While Russia did not formally denounce the 2010 Demarcation Agreement, its prime utility henceforth was to invoke it as a basis for attacking Ukraine's efforts to demarcate its borders unilaterally (Zhurzhenko, 2021).

Maritime borders

Ukraine's maritime border with Russia – as inherited from the Ukrainian SSR – extends from the Black Sea south of the Kerch Strait, through the Kerch Strait, and into the Azov Sea. During the Soviet era, the Azov Sea and the Kerch Strait were considered waters internal to a single state (Schatz and Koval, 2019). Thus, they were the exclusive domain of neither the RSFSR nor the Ukrainian SSR, with questions of access, navigation and exploitation determined centrally by the Soviet authorities. Following Ukraine's independence, there appeared two states bordering the Azov Sea and the Kerch Strait, raising questions about their legal status.

Consistent with its efforts to consolidate its political independence, Ukraine's preference was for treating the sea as international waters. Accordingly, Kyiv wanted to proceed with the delineation of territorial waters and jurisdictions into the national sectors of two sovereign states. This entailed sovereignty over territorial waters within 12 nautical miles of Ukraine's coastline, and jurisdiction over the contiguous zone (the area of sea extending a further 12 miles beyond the territorial waters) and an exclusive economic zone according to international maritime law, a position which Ukraine declared to the UN in 1992 (Ustymenko, 2024).

Russia's preference, however, was to preserve the status quo, continuing to treat the Azov Sea as 'internal waters'. Moscow was particularly concerned with securing control over the Kerch-Yeni-Kale Channel (KEC), representing the western deep and most navigable part of the Kerch Strait. The KEC had been entrusted to the management of the Ukrainian SSR in 1988, and Ukraine deemed it an unquestionable part of its territory as an independent state.[8] To further its aims, Russia insisted that the legal status and regime of use of the sea and the strait should be addressed as a single whole, thereby ensuring that both areas retained the status of internal waters and were used jointly by Russia and Ukraine without any delimitation of maritime spaces.[9] To this end, for example, Moscow proposed the formation of a bilateral Azov Sea Council.[10] Given Russia's naval superiority such a solution would have allowed Moscow to formalize its preponderance in the basin, a prospect Ukraine was unwilling to accept.

Despite repeated talks, no progress was made in bridging the positions of Russia and Ukraine. Even though Moscow

8 In 1999, Ukraine proclaimed a boundary line in the Kerch Strait which put the island of Tuzla on the Ukrainian side (Schatz and Koval, 2019).

9 Protocol of talks, https://zakon.rada.gov.ua/laws/show/643_236/print.

10 https://jamestown.org/program/russia-demands-azov-sea-condominium-with-ukraine/

offered Ukraine's leadership the carrot of the 2003 State Border Agreement, this gesture of goodwill did not extend to maritime borders. Despite its name, the agreement defined only state *land* borders. Faced with Moscow's recalcitrance, the Ukrainian side pressed for a commitment to the future resolution of the issue (Musafirova, 2023). Kyiv succeeded in getting Russia to agree that matters related to 'adjacent sea waters' would be addressed in a separate agreement 'in accordance with international law'. The Ukrainian negotiators hoped that the use of the word 'adjacent' (*smezhnye*) would imply the existence of boundaries (*mezhi*), which the reference to international law would affirm. However, the Russian side countered this insertion with a provision stating that any future arrangement would be made notwithstanding the status of the sea and the strait as 'internal waters of both states'. This was a clear win for Moscow and demonstrated its ability to prevail upon Ukraine's political leaders in the early 2000s.

Kuchma's vulnerability, however, gave Russia the opportunity to go beyond advancing its preferences by expanding the scope for legal ambiguity. Moscow moved to change the facts on the ground and assert its territorial claims by targeting Tuzla, a sandy islet in the Kerch Strait of about 0.7 km^2, situated just a few hundred metres from the Crimean peninsula. In September 2003, Moscow began construction work to link Russia's Taman peninsula with Tuzla. This amounted to a de facto annexation of Tuzla, as it would have allowed Moscow to shift the border westward and thereby take control of the KEC (Socor, 2018a). In doing so, Moscow rejected both Ukraine's factual and legal justifications for Tuzla as an island and part of Ukrainian territory.[11] In response, Ukraine acted

[11] Russia claimed the island was a split and that it was originally linked to Taman, but a fairway was made by local fishermen to avoid having to sail round the island (Skaridov, 2014).

swiftly, deploying troops to the island and threatening to derail Russia's renewed integration plans for Ukraine (see Chapter 6).

In order to de-escalate the situation, Kyiv and Moscow signed a new agreement on cooperation in the use of the Azov Sea and the Kerch Strait in December 2003, which appeared to resolve the issue. Yet, capitalizing on its brazen move to incorporate Tuzla, and on Kuchma's political weakness at the time, Russia gave nothing away, merely halting the construction work it had initiated. In exchange, Moscow secured another legally vague accord, which further eroded Ukraine's sovereignty.

To start with, the brief accord – consisting of only five articles – did not resolve the legal status of the Azov Sea and the Kerch Strait. In line with Russia's preference, it affirmed that the sea and the strait represented 'historically internal waters'. To placate Ukraine, the agreement stipulated that delimitation would take place in the future, yet nothing in the text indicated any genuine intention on Russia's part to commence such a process in the future.[12] Furthermore, unlike the State Border Agreement, this deal made no mention of the applicability of international law, even in its Preamble, thereby weakening Ukraine's ability to invoke international law conventions in the future. Thus, the result was another example of 'legal vacuums covered by Russian-composed legal formulae, whereby Russia de facto holds sway' (Socor, 2018a).

Instead, Russia focused on the terms of the 'use' of the Azov Sea and the Kerch Strait to ensure its preponderance. Accordingly, the deal allowed the free passage of Russian and Ukrainian commercial and military vessels. However, the lack of detailed provisions ensured that Russian ships could roam freely, conduct exercises or approach the Ukrainian shore without violating any agreement (Socor, 2018a). Commercial

12 For example, there was no agreement on baseline or starting coastal points or the basis for a delimitation methodology to be used in the future (Skaridov, 2014).

vessels of third countries were allowed to enter the strait only if navigating to a Russian or Ukrainian port. Non-commercial vessels required an invitation or permission from the port, coordinated with the other party. Unsurprisingly, the agreement made no provision regarding the specific terms of such permissions. As a result, the deal enshrined Russia's right to object to third-party access, thereby strengthening its control in the Black Sea basin.

Finally, the agreement provided for strict bilateral resolution of disputes. In combination with the absence of a reference to international law, this amounted to carving out a *sui generis* 'internal' regime, leaving Ukraine vulnerable to Russian pressure, which was soon to be applied. Ukraine was bound by yet another precarious deal, open to unilateral interpretation by a party that had already demonstrated its willingness to encroach on Ukraine's territorial integrity.

Cashing in on the uncertainty

Unsurprisingly, the delimitation of the maritime border was not on the agenda in Moscow. Faced with Moscow's intransigence on the issue, and mindful of the legal trap that Kuchma had fallen into in 2003, the Yushchenko administration (2005–9) requested a revision of the Azov Sea agreement in the summer of 2006. Kyiv objected to the designation of the sea as internal waters, renewing its call for it to be treated as an international sea, with clearly defined zones of national jurisdiction under international law. These efforts, however, proved fruitless.

The situation did not improve under the presidency of the pro-Russian Yanukovych. As with the land borders, Russia merely dangled the prospect of addressing maritime borders.[13]

[13] This time, however, it only signalled an intention in a Joint Statement of 12 July 2012, rather than signing an agreement, http://kremlin.ru/supplement/1259.

The stalemate became the new normal, with numerous incidents underscoring Russia's determination to consolidate its de facto control over the basin.[14] Any demands from Ukraine to establish routine inter-state relations regarding borders were denounced as unreasonable, as violations of the vague and imprecise agreements, and as unfriendly acts toward Russia.

Following the annexation of Crimea in March 2014, Moscow gained full control over the Kerch Strait. It began the construction of a bridge linking the Taman and Kerch peninsulas, which was completed in May 2018. The bridge provided a vital physical link between Russia and Crimea, reducing the latter's dependence on Ukraine, but it also became an important mechanism for restricting Ukraine's free passage through the strait. Construction itself temporarily restricted access, with Ukraine vehemently protesting the violation of the free navigation principle of the 2003 agreement, albeit unsuccessfully (Schatz and Koval, 2019). The height of the Kerch Strait bridge limited vessel height to 33 metres, thereby restricting the size of ships able to enter the Sea of Azov and reach Ukrainian ports (Gressel, 2021). This also resulted in a de facto blockade of two of Ukraine's major mainland ports – Mariupol and Berdyansk – with severe economic consequences.

At the same time, Russia introduced a border control regime for the strait, increasing the transit time of vessels, and facilitating the harassment and detention of Ukrainian ships. Moscow moved to directly limit Ukraine's maritime movements. In what became the gravest incident, in November 2018, a Ukrainian tugboat and a group of patrol craft attempted to pass through the Kerch Strait into the Sea of Azov. They were attacked, boarded and captured while still in international waters by the Russian navy, before even coming close to the Kerch Strait. Having detained 23 Ukrainian

[14] For example, in July 2013 Russian Coast Guards destroyed a Ukrainian fishing boat for illegal fishing on 'Russian territory' (Skaridov, 2014).

sailors, Moscow claimed that they had illegally entered Russian territorial waters.

It is notable that the 2003 Azov Sea and Kerch Strait Agreement provided Russia with the necessary legal cover to justify its coercive actions in the Azov Sea and Kerch Strait. Moscow argued that the part of the agreement relating to the Kerch Strait was no longer binding, as the strait was now exclusively Russian and not a shared waterway. This gave it the right to build across the strait and also patrol or restrict access by both Ukrainian and international vessels. At the same time, however, it claimed that the agreement confirmed the Azov Sea as shared internal waters, thus asserting its own right to move freely and approach any coastal areas at will. Indeed, in so far as it served Russia's interests, the Kremlin insisted that the deal could not be denounced by either side.[15]

As the events attracted some – albeit largely rhetorical – international condemnation (Lewis, 2019), Russia's Foreign Ministry stepped forward to explain that Moscow was exercising its legitimate rights in a non-discriminatory manner (Socor, 2018a; Schatz and Koval, 2019). Yet, as Socor observed, 'the rules ... seemed to be what Russia says they are. Russia is in a position unilaterally to determine which treaty provisions no longer apply at all since 2014, or apply partly or selectively, or yet apply from time to time on a case-by-case basis' (2018a). Such legal instrumentalism yet again provided leverage that Moscow could use to exert pressure on Ukraine at its discretion (see Chapter 7).

In 2018, Ukraine protested that 'further creeping annexation ... is taking place', but Kyiv found itself in a legal limbo, unable to resort to international remedies.[16] Notably, Russia

15 The agreement was finally denounced by both parties only in the spring and summer of 2023.

16 Ukraine's Navy Chief Ihor Voronchencko, speaking in July 2018 (cited in Atland, 2021: 307).

refused to extend any international format – such as the Normandy-format discussions or OSCE missions – to address developments in the Kerch-Azov region. Moscow asserted that the proposals for observation or mediation were unnecessary, claiming that 'the solution is that the rules of passage should strictly be respected' (Socor, 2018b). Ukraine sought to enforce its rights before the Permanent Court of Arbitration and the International Tribunal for the Law of the Sea in 2016 and 2018, respectively, but Russia responded by challenging the authority of these bodies and arguing that the issues fell under domestic law enforcement (Atland, 2021). Russia's selective invocation of legal agreements made clear its intent to operate with a free hand, beyond the reach of international oversight.

Ultimately, Moscow deemed itself unconstrained by technicalities, preparing for the escalation of its strategy. Further incidents followed. For example, in the spring of 2021 Moscow fully blocked access to the Sea of Azov, citing 'military manoeuvres' as justification for banning all but Russian naval vessels from approaching the Kerch Strait. Even after the manoeuvres concluded, Russia maintained the restrictions, effectively cutting off Ukrainian access to its ports. These actions undermined Ukraine's navigation rights, inflicted economic damage through lost revenue and trade, disrupted international traffic, and helped lay the groundwork for the full-scale invasion of 2022.

Conclusions

Delineating borders is a fundamental aspect of defining and consolidating statehood. On the face of it, Ukraine left the USSR with the territory and borders as they existed in 1991. But, as our analysis indicates, Russia was hardly ready to accept Ukraine's borders and sought to keep them 'open' and, when Ukraine refused, it attempted to derail Ukraine's plans in a variety of ways. The delayed start to border negotiations and the limited progress made betrayed Russia's profound reluctance to help alleviate Ukraine's deep-seated concerns. This was a way of undermining Ukraine's efforts to fully consolidate its territorial sovereignty and instead perpetuate Russia's control. While nominally complying with the international legal commitments, namely the unconditional recognition of Ukrainian independence and sovereignty, Moscow blocked the very creation of the basic features of this sovereignty: the recognition, delimitation and demarcation of borders.

By 2003, this strategy resulted in an overt challenge to the territorial integrity of Ukraine. With this step, a seed was planted that presented Russia with a bountiful yield in 2014. The international agreement that was meant to resolve border issues became a prime tool for depriving Ukraine of its economic and political sovereignty in the sea. While the Ukrainians knew better, Western observers grossly underestimated the significance of the 2003 and 2018 incidents. The analysis of Russia's approach to Ukraine's borders amply illustrates how law was instrumentalized to limit Ukraine's sovereignty and territorial integrity well before the full-scale invasion in 2022.

SIX

Back to the Union? Russia's Projects to Attract Ukraine

At the end of 1991, Yeltsin's Russia reluctantly recognized Ukraine's independence, operating under the assumption that it would be a short-lived state of affairs. Russia hoped to manage Ukraine's independence within a new formal structure designed to promote unity and cooperation among the post-Soviet countries. Establishing a formal union – albeit significantly much looser than the USSR – offered several advantages. As argued in Chapter 3, such a union would reinforce the narrative of the consensual dissolution of the USSR and bolster international support for Russia's claim to the lion's share of the Soviet legacy. Domestically, it would help placate discontent and neo-imperialist pressures over the loss of Ukraine, signalling that it had not truly departed from the patrimony despite its nominal sovereignty. The new union would facilitate a gradual and peaceful reversal of the perceived 'anomaly' of Ukraine's statehood by ensuring its participation in an open-ended process of integration with Russia, however vaguely defined at the outset. Moreover, the creation of joint institutions under the union framework would replicate the well-established Soviet formula for constraining Ukraine's autonomy. A formal union would thus provide Russia with both the legal façade of respecting Ukraine's sovereignty and a set of instruments to assert its entitlement over Kyiv.

This chapter demonstrates how the pursuit of formal unity remained a strategic objective for Russia over the subsequent decades, even as the formats through which Moscow pursued this goal evolved continuously (see Table 6.1). Russia was notably proactive in initiating repeated reintegration efforts. By most accounts, no other state has proposed as many treaties across diverse sectors – including economy, energy and security – as Russia (Busygina and Filippov, 2021: 47).

Under Yeltsin, reintegration plans remained vague and disparate, as Russia struggled to devise a workable framework for re-engaging the post-Soviet countries. While various multilateral formats were initiated, Moscow's interests were best served through bilateral arrangements for 'partnership and cooperation'. These allowed Russia to exploit Ukraine's political and economic dependence and to cultivate segments of the Ukrainian elite. However, this bilateral strategy proved insufficient to secure Russia's control or to restrict Ukraine's direct engagement with Western states and organizations. Bilateral agreements failed to provide Russia with a robust

Table 6.1: Russia's integration projects and Ukraine's responses to them

Organization/initiative	Ukraine's response
CIS (1991)	Engagement in selected CIS agreements; not a member according to the 1993 CIS Charter
CIS Economic Union (1993)	Associate member; treaty not ratified
Customs Union (1995, upgrades in 1996 and 1999)	Refused participation
Eurasian Economic Community (2000)	Observer
Common Economic Space (2003)	Full member but conditional on compliance with the Constitution; backtracked
Eurasian Customs Union (2010, upgrade in 2011)	Refused participation in Spring 2011; observer in autumn 2013

position and a legitimate rationale for regional dominance, thereby undermining its broader global ambitions. In response, Moscow embraced the concept of 'modern regionalism', a thinly veiled but internationally palatable justification for renewed efforts to assert patrimonial control in the post-Soviet space.

Upon assuming power in 2000, Vladimir Putin sought to reverse the geopolitical consequences of the USSR's dissolution, which had diminished both Russia's patrimony and its global status. Domestic consolidation of power was pursued in tandem with efforts to establish a formal and functional union. Securing Ukraine's inclusion in this new Russia-led integration bloc was central to this strategy. Accordingly, Putin demanded Ukraine's unconditional, full and binding membership. The sheer volume of initiatives aimed at achieving this objective reflects the intensity and persistence of Russian efforts, as well as the fixation of its political elite. Ultimately, Eurasian integration also demonstrated the limits of Ukraine's sovereignty as Russia sought to enforce its perceived entitlement over Ukraine, especially in opposition to external actors, such as the EU (Dragneva and Wolczuk, 2015a).

The CIS episode

As outlined in Chapter 3, Yeltsin was eager to maintain some form of union among the post-Soviet states – particularly Belarus and Ukraine. Confronted with Ukraine's resistance, Yeltsin agreed in December 1991 to the only arrangement acceptable to Kyiv: the CIS. Legally, the CIS – as constituted through the ad hoc negotiations at Byelavezha – was far removed from a union or even a loose confederation. It lacked permanent common institutions or clear membership rules, and operated entirely within the framework of international law (Dragneva, 2004).

This format proved problematic. While it nominally formalized the dissolution of the USSR, it left Russia with few institutional mechanisms for control over the increasingly assertive newly independent states. For some, the CIS symbolized Russia's retreat from its historical sphere of control in favour of improved relations with the West, while tolerating 'the provocative and irritating pranks of fledgling statehood' of the former union republics 'hurrying to convince the world of the reality of their independence'.[1]

Although Moscow remained committed to reintegration, it lacked a coherent strategy for reassembling the Soviet successor states into a new Russia-led union. Politically, the concept of 'near abroad' was used to delineate a region where Russia claimed distinct rights and responsibilities, framed as 'special' rather than 'imperial' (see Chapter 1). To this end, Moscow sought to strengthen the CIS as an international organization. In January 1993 the Charter of the CIS was adopted, establishing rules of membership and creating formal bodies, including a permanently functioning executive, a Coordination and Consultative Committee, and an Economic Court.[2] Despite the ongoing adjustments to the organization's structure,[3] the reforms failed to address the fundamental deficiencies of the initial design produced at Byelavezha (Dragneva, 2004).

From an economic perspective, Russia's 'special' role had to be balanced against the financial burden of subsidizing the other republics, at the very time when Moscow urgently needed to prioritize its own economic reform. Thus, Moscow was keen to invest in a union – or at least secure the future commitment to one – but simultaneously sought to minimize its economic

1 'Russian neighbours urged to sign border treaties', *Rossiyskaya Gazeta*, 12 June 1992 (in Brzezinski and Sullivan, 1997: 91).

2 The Economic Court of the CIS was already set up in July 1992. An Inter-Parliamentary Assembly was created in March 1992, but was not incorporated in the CIS Charter.

3 Most notably in 1998 when Yeltsin's economic backer Boris Berezovsky was appointed as Executive Secretary of the CIS, and in April 1999 when several bodies were merged into a CIS Executive Committee.

costs and maximize its own discretion to act unilaterally. As Yeltsin stated, 'integration must not bring harm to Russia itself or lead to overstretch of our forces and resources, material as well as financial' (cited in Jonson, 2004: 44).

This 'neo-isolationist' position was soon challenged by the proponents of a common economic area, including Yevgeny Primakov, Director of the Foreign Intelligence Service, who viewed it as 'virtually the only way of reducing tension in interstate relations'.[4] In Moscow, it was believed that

> [T]he Russia ruble and Russian energy sources will successfully replace the general secretary of the Communist Party. This will be an empire of a 'new type', a 'velvet' empire, that establishes itself on the financial-economic and military dependence of the post-Soviet republics on Russia and, owing to this, that ensures the political hegemony of Russia in the post-Soviet space.[5]

The example of the EU, newly upgraded by the 1992 Treaty of Maastricht, provided an ideal role model for enacting these ambitions. In 1993 Moscow set out to create an Economic Union, drawing inspiration from the EU common market. The common market formula provided a legitimate framework for reasserting Russia's regional role, combining ambitious, far-reaching objectives with a gradual, staged approach to achieve it. It enabled Russia to seek an open-ended commitment to a future union from other post-Soviet states. The initial stages, such as the establishment of a free trade area, were presented as transitional steps.[6] In this way, Moscow could secure political

4 'Text of FIS report presented by Primakov', *Rossiyskaya Gazeta*, 22 September 1994 (in Brzezinski and Sullivan, 1997: 111).

5 'Moscow's CIS policy changes assessed', *Nezavisimaya Gazeta*, 9 February 1995 (in Brzezinski and Sullivan, 1997: 141).

6 Indeed, the CIS FTA signed in April 1994 was defined as a first step toward the creation of an Economic Union.

loyalty and geopolitical control via economic integration, while minimizing its own costs. To attract participation, Russia signed the CIS-wide free trade agreements in 1994 and in 1999, yet never ratified them. Instead, Moscow managed relations on a bilateral basis, allowing greater flexibility to leverage its own commitments for political goals (Dragneva and de Kort, 2007; Cooper, 2009).

This strategy proved only partially effective. Although the CIS developed some institutional structure, it remained a fragmented and ineffective format. Faced with limited progress within the CIS, Russia shifted its focus to smaller cooperative frameworks that could serve as an integration vanguard, with the expectation that other CIS members might eventually join.[7] To this end, in January 1995 Russia signed an agreement on a customs union with Belarus and Kazakhstan, later joined by Kyrgyzstan (1997) and Tajikistan (1998). Despite Moscow's intentions to deepen cooperation,[8] these initiatives had very little practical impact. Nevertheless, they marked a significant shift in Russia's approach toward pursuing closer economic integration with a smaller, more select group of states.

Ukraine's resistance

For Moscow, Ukraine's participation in a new union was a coveted goal. However, it was consistently undermined by Kyiv's repeated refusal to commit to any project perceived as compromising Ukraine's sovereignty. From Ukraine's perspective, Russia's integration efforts represented a vehicle for reasserting regional hegemony at the expense of Ukrainian independence. These concerns were exacerbated by Russia's

[7] These were treaty regimes embedded within the CIS rather than establishing a new international organization.

[8] In March 1996, an Agreement on Deepening Integration in the Economic and Humanitarian Areas was signed, followed by another Treaty on the Customs Union and the Single Economic Space of February 1999.

ongoing challenges to Ukraine's territorial integrity, reinforcing Kyiv's opposition to the institutional consolidation of the CIS. Notably, Kyiv declined participation in the permanent institutions established in 1992, such as the Inter-Parliamentary Assembly and the Economic Court of the CIS. Kyiv's resistance to institutional constraints was further demonstrated by its categorical refusal to sign the CIS Charter adopted in January 1993. As a result, Ukraine never became a member of the organization in legal terms (Dragneva, 2004). Kyiv committed to setting up permanent executives of the CIS, but only with reservations attached to the relevant agreements.[9] While Ukraine was interested in economic cooperation within the CIS framework, it found the design of the 1993 Economic Union overly open-ended and, therefore, too far-reaching. Consequently, it joined only as an associate member.

Recognizing the limitations of the CIS-wide model, Moscow sought to involve Ukraine in smaller formats for cooperation, such as the 1995 Customs Union. At the time, Moscow was optimistic, particularly following the election of President Kuchma, who championed more pragmatic relations with Russia and criticized the Ukrainian nationalists who overlooked the country's economic dependence on Russia (Wolczuk, 1997). Framed in explicitly economic terms, these initiatives promised Ukraine improved market access and more favourable energy pricing from Russia. Russia, however, was keen to capitalize on the political symbolism of such economic initiatives and use them as instruments of political reintegration. In addition to political overtures, the Russian leadership

[9] That is the Consultative and Coordination Committee set up in 1993. Ukraine took a similar stand regarding the Executive Committee and Economic Council set up in 1999. The only nominal concession was made in 1998 when Ukraine conceded to joining the largely symbolic Inter-Parliamentary Assembly in order to help secure Russia's ratification of the 1997 Friendship Treaty and, thereby, the unconditional recognition of Ukraine's territorial integrity.

reinforced its strategy with economic pressure. Specifically, Moscow imposed excise duties on oil and gas exports to Ukraine until Kyiv agreed to join the Customs Union, thereby increasing the cost of remaining outside it (Balmaceda, 1998).

Despite President Kuchma's initial pledge to 'normalize' relations with Russia, he soon grew wary of the political and economic costs associated with Moscow's demands. His stance reflected the preferences of his political and economic base, particularly regional elites in eastern and southern Ukraine, who wanted free trade with Russia and the CIS but remained cautious about deeper political reintegration (Bukkvoll, 2004). Like his predecessor, Leonid Kravchuk, Kuchma was sceptical of the political objectives underpinning Russia's integration initiatives and questioned the credibility of Moscow's promises. Consequently, he resisted participation in the Customs Union. Instead, Kuchma called for the full implementation of existing commitments, before considering any further steps toward integration.

This cautious engagement – entering into dialogue on Russia's regional projects while ultimately eschewing participation – became a hallmark of Kuchma's two terms as president (1994–2004). It constituted an 'integration game' that Ukraine played with Russia, aimed at maximising the benefits of cooperation, while limiting its own obligations due to the deep-seated distrust of Russia's intentions (Dragneva and Wolczuk, 2015a).

The default option of bilateral 'partnership and cooperation'

Paradoxically, Ukraine's limited, highly selective engagement with the CIS and its various off-shoots provided Russia with bilateral means to secure Ukraine's loyalty by exploiting its political vulnerability and economic needs. Russia relied on this method in the lead-up to the 1997 Treaty on Friendship, Cooperation and Partnership.

For Ukraine, the treaty embodied the long-sought formal recognition of its sovereignty and territorial integrity. Kyiv had invested considerable diplomatic effort in securing such legal guarantees from Russia through a general political agreement. The new treaty was intended to replace the outdated Friendship Agreement of 1990, which had ambiguously linked territorial integrity to continued union membership, as discussed in Chapter 3. The 1997 deal appeared to affirm Ukraine's sovereignty in legal terms, seemingly outside the framework of any formal union. On the surface, Ukraine's position had prevailed. However, Russia used the treaty negotiations as an opportunity to advance reintegration efforts under the guise of bilateral cooperation. A close reading of the treaty reveals that more than half of its provisions institutionalized extensive cooperation with Russia, thereby embedding mechanisms that fell short of formal union but nonetheless served Moscow's strategic interests.

It is indicative that as part of the 1997 agreement, Ukraine demonstrated a degree of openness to commitments Kyiv had previously rejected within the CIS-wide format. These included the staged formation of a single economic space and the deepening of integration across a broad range of policy areas (Article 13). While the precise nature of Ukraine's undertakings may be subject to interpretation, given the nuances of legal drafting, the agreement nonetheless marked a significant achievement for Russia's coercive diplomacy. The treaty outlined measures for defence, industrial and energy cooperation, thereby binding Ukraine to existing business networks and reviving historical interdependencies in these strategic sectors (Sherr, 1997).

In this context, the bilateral 'partnership and cooperation' framework offered the second-best avenue for Russia to enact its control over Ukraine. By capitalizing on Kyiv's selective interests, Moscow reinforced its extra-legal leverage and promoted economic unity by harnessing dependence. However, these efforts remained tentative. During the first decade of Ukrainian independence, Russia lacked a coordinated political strategy toward Ukraine (Bukkvoll, 2001). This would change with the coming to power of Vladimir Putin in 2000.

Putin and the search for a new union

Upon assuming office, Putin made clear his ambition to re-establish Russia as a great power within the international system (Sherr, 2002). Creating a regional organization to reunite the lost patrimony became key to achieve this vision. As ever, Ukraine's participation remained central to Moscow's plans. Crucially, Putin's domestic political consolidation enabled a more assertive and coordinated approach than had been possible under Yeltsin.

Recognizing the CIS failures, Putin initiated the creation of the Eurasian Economic Community (EEC) in October 2000. This project built on the earlier sub-regional, loose treaty regime, transforming it into an internationally recognized organization. The EEC was endowed with developed common bodies and, above all, an international legal personality. Given Moscow's underlying political motivations, such internal and external institutional actorness was essential. Despite the nod to institutional equality, Russia ensured its dominance within the decision-making structures of the organization (Dragneva, 2013). Like its predecessors in the 1990s, the EEC was conceived as an open-ended project, aiming at far-reaching cooperation across a broad spectrum of policy areas, as determined by its highest body – the Interstate Council. It seemed that Russia finally had a union it could use to 'manage' its region.

Putin's team actively pursued Ukraine's membership, perfecting Yeltsin's approach of combining threats with enticements. Moscow employed a blend of extensive trade and energy benefits, tailored to the priorities and vulnerabilities of the Ukrainian political elites (Dragneva and Wolczuk, 2015a, 2016). For instance, Putin extended crucial political support to

President Kuchma during the fallout from the Gongadze affair, which had strained Kyiv's relations with Western partners. Kyiv remained wary of compromising its sovereignty and resisted full membership. Yet, hoping it could still reap the benefits, Russia was willing to pay for Ukraine's participation and in May 2002 Kuchma agreed to join the EEC as an observer.

However, this level of engagement fell decidedly short of the Kremlin's expectations. Even though the EEC stumbled on, a new initiative – the Common Economic Space (CES) – was proposed in February 2003. Presented in strictly economic terms, the CES was designed as a multi-speed framework, reflecting Russia's willingness to accommodate Ukraine's preferences. Nevertheless, its underlying political objective – to rebind Ukraine within a formal union with Moscow – was unmistakable. The CES envisioned deep economic integration, including a currency union and a robust common regulatory authority (Kembayev, 2009).

In Ukraine these proposals sparked intense domestic debate, both among political elites and within the expert community.[10] Given its vague objectives, accession to the CES was seen as an open-ended commitment to reintegration with Russia. The CES was depicted as a 'return to the USSR' and relegation to 'the second division of Europe' by Roman Shpek, Ukraine's representative to the EU (Poliakova, 2003). Russia made free trade concessions conditional upon Ukraine's commitment to deeper integration, which raised concerns about the potential erosion of Ukraine's sovereignty and the violation of explicit constitutional prohibitions enshrined in the 1996 Constitution. Kuchma's oligarchic backers were eager to secure access to

[10] For example, see Center for Peace, Conversion and Foreign Policy of Ukraine, Experts' evaluation on the Draft Agreement, 1 September 2003. A study on Ukraine's Eurasian vector conducted by the Razumkov Centre was also reported in *Zerkalo Nedeli*, 27 December 2002, https://zn.ua/business/ukraina__evrazes_nablyudenie_sotrudnichestvo_integratsiya.html.

the Russian market, yet they also feared the resulting loss of 'economic sovereignty' (Bukkvoll, 2004).

With the end of Kuchma's second presidential term approaching, the incumbent elites faced growing uncertainty surrounding the 2004 presidential election. This vulnerability prompted Kuchma to enlist Russian support and, in return, show increased willingness to accept Moscow's demands regarding the CES (Bukkvoll, 2004). In February 2003, Kuchma signed a joint declaration on the CES, which culminated in a founding agreement in September. This agreement was ratified by the Ukrainian parliament in April 2004, just six months before the presidential election. The process was led by Kuchma's special envoy, Deputy Prime Minister Mykola Azarov, known for his pro-Russian stance, and was conducted in an expedited and opaque manner, bypassing standard governmental procedures and alienating the political opposition (Dragneva and Wolczuk, 2015a).

At the time, Putin's strategy appeared successful, as it secured Ukraine's signature on the agreement, despite widespread domestic resistance. The Kremlin's strategy of linking economic benefits to reintegration proved most effective when the political survival of Ukraine's elites depended on Russian economic and political support. However, this success proved superficial. Although the general CES agreement allowed Moscow to interpret its provisions in line with its own strategic vision, it also afforded Kuchma (and his successor) considerable flexibility in managing relations with Russia. Crucially, Kuchma signed the agreement with a key reservation: Ukraine's participation must not contravene the 1996 Constitution. Even when beleaguered by domestic politics, the Ukrainian leadership drew a fine line between 'strategic partnership' and integration with Russia, particularly in light of renewed threats to Ukraine's territorial integrity. As discussed in Chapter 5, the Tuzla incident served as a stark reminder to Ukraine's political elite of the risks posed by Russia. In response to this overt challenge to Ukraine's sovereignty, Kuchma announced that

Ukraine had not made a definitive commitment to integration, and that any future steps would depend on the establishment of a functioning free trade area (Bukkvoll, 2004).

The banner of Eurasian regionalism

Kuchma failed to transfer power to his designated successor, Viktor Yanukovych, who had received overt support from Russia. The mass protests against electoral fraud, known as the Orange Revolution of 2004, paved the way for the election of Viktor Yushchenko as president (2005–9). This marked a watershed moment in Ukraine–Russia relations. Until then, the Kremlin had operated under the assumption that Ukraine's political orientation would remain favourably disposed toward Russia. Although Kuchma and the oligarchs had resisted full compliance with Russia's integration agenda, they had not dismissed Moscow's demands outright. Furthermore, it was to Moscow's advantage that Ukraine under Kuchma was not perceived as a particularly attractive partner for Western engagement (Wolczuk, 2019). In contrast, the post-Orange Revolution leadership reoriented Ukraine decisively toward the West, explicitly seeking closer ties with the EU, including membership. In pursuit of this aim, Kyiv was ready to enter legally binding commitments leading to open-ended, comprehensive integration with the EU.

Thus, by 2005 it had become evident that Moscow's existing regional strategy was failing to yield the desired outcomes. None of the established integration frameworks had achieved meaningful progress or secured Ukraine's formal commitment. Post-Orange Ukraine was effectively defaulting on its loyalty to Russia. Despite Ukraine's prior tradition of declarative Europeanization (Wolczuk, 2009), the Orange Revolution created a genuine opening for integration with the EU, an outcome perceived in Moscow as Europe's encroachment on Russia's patrimony. Although the EU did not endorse

Ukraine's membership aspirations, it agreed to negotiate a new enhanced agreement aimed at fostering economic integration and political cooperation. Negotiations on the Association Agreement commenced in 2007, followed by talks on its economic component, the Deep and Comprehensive Free Trade Area (DCFTA), in 2008, after Ukraine's accession to the World Trade Organization. These developments underscored the need for Moscow to devise a new strategy and adopt a revised approach to reverse this dynamic. The strengthening of Ukraine's partnership with NATO and the launch of the EU's Eastern Partnership initiative in 2009 further heightened the Kremlin's sense of urgency.

Once again, regional integration provided a ready-made framing for Russia's efforts, which Moscow embraced with renewed vigour. While some economic benefits were anticipated from regional economic integration, it was the political and geopolitical implications that held the greatest appeal for Russia (Dragneva and Wolczuk, 2013). At its core, effective region-building served as a source of power, a means of appropriating what Jupille and Jolliff (2011: 13) describe as the 'latest pre-requisite for membership in today's international political script of modernity'. Within such regional project, Russia could dominate any common bodies either by design or, given its size and relative power, by default.

Furthermore, 'deep' integration, characterized by market and regulatory alignment and the adoption of common policies, would erect barriers to the entry of external actors. At the very least, it would ensure that any engagement with such actors would be negotiated at the intra-bloc level, in accordance with Moscow's preferences. Crucially, this could be achieved while deflecting accusations of neo-imperialism. Framed as a modern, functional initiative for economic integration, the project could be presented as analogous to European integration. In this narrative, Russia was a 'normal' power, partaking in global trends of integration, globalization and interdependence (Dragneva and Wolczuk, 2015b).

Given the stakes in Ukraine, Russia was prepared to invest in a new integration initiative. By the summer of 2010, it had successfully launched a customs union with Belarus and Kazakhstan, underpinned by a legal and institutional framework exhibiting distinctive supranational features (Dragneva, 2013). Despite its problems, this looked like a promising platform for economic integration. However, the Kremlin's priority was not the consolidation of these achievements or the careful implementation of its complex agenda. Instead, its principal objective remained the rapid reunification of what it perceived as its patrimony. Unlike the gradual process of European integration, Russia pursued its regional project with considerable speed. By early 2011, plans were already under way to transform the Customs Union into a Eurasian Union, a new international organization (Cooper, 2013). Unsurprisingly, Ukraine's participation was once again placed at the forefront of Moscow's agenda.

This time, Ukraine was headed by Viktor Yanukovych, elected in early 2010 on a pro-Russian platform. Yanukovych quickly proved amenable to Russian interests, agreeing to extend the lease of the Sevastopol naval base as part of a gas deal. In return, Ukraine received a 30 per cent discount on the 2009 gas pricing formula (see Chapter 4).[11] With the Kremlin's strategy of exploiting Ukraine's energy vulnerability proving effective, Moscow escalated its demands.

This time Russia aimed to achieve what had eluded it since 1991: Ukraine's full and unconditional membership in an open-ended Russia-led union with strong common bodies (Dragneva and Wolczuk, 2015a). This ambition persisted despite Ukraine's ongoing pursuit of deep economic integration

[11] In effect, Russia obtained the political benefits of the Kharkiv deal but gave little away: the pricing formula, even after the 'political discount', still meant that Ukraine was paying more for imports than EU countries such as Germany or Italy, despite the higher transit costs of the latter.

with the EU on a bilateral basis. Moscow's determination and disregard of Ukraine's sovereignty was on full display as Russian senior politicians warned Kyiv against invoking constitutional constraints to limit its commitments (Glaz'ev, 2011).

Drawing on the narrative of regional integration, Moscow set out to sway Ukraine 'nicely': by spelling out the functional benefits for Ukraine. The Kremlin sought to sweeten the deal by pledging to resolve long-standing issues related to market access, energy and sectoral cooperation, areas that had consistently strained bilateral relations. These promises were particularly attractive to Yanukovych's oligarchic supporters, who viewed sustained energy and trade dependence as a viable substitute for the domestic reforms they were reluctant to pursue.

Russia's strategy targeted Ukraine's rent-seeking elites, making it clear that failure to comply would result in extensive trade penalties. Moreover, Moscow did not hesitate to invoke threats concerning unresolved border disputes in the Azov–Kerch region (Sidorenko, 2011).

Despite the intensive campaign, Yanukovych, like his predecessors, rejected membership. Ukrainian officials and experts remained sceptical, not only about the economic costs and benefits but also about the scope of Russia's demands and intentions (Dragneva and Wolczuk, 2015a). The 2010 Kharkiv deal had left Yanukovych bruised and cautious: Kyiv was acutely aware of the low credibility of Russia's promises and its propensity to extract concessions without delivering the promised rewards. Ukraine's elites were equally conscious of the Kremlin's increasing willingness to act on its threats. Russia's interventions across the region, particularly the 2008 war with Georgia, had dispelled any lingering illusions about Moscow's sentimental ties to its former 'Soviet brothers'.

However, counting on Ukraine's geopolitical significance for Russia, Yanukovych hoped that he could satisfy Moscow by engaging in alternative formats under the banner of 'strategic economic partnership' with Russia.

Fighting the Ukraine–EU Association Agreement

For Moscow, the prospect of Ukraine signing an association agreement with the EU was, above all, perceived as a direct challenge to Russia's presumed rights over Ukraine. Just as Russia had historically used agreements and trade mechanisms to mask subordination and pursue political goals, so it interpreted the EU's efforts to promote modernization and integration as an encroachment on 'its' region. While the EU indulged in technocratic and legalistic detail, for Moscow the agreement was about the rivalry over its patrimony, plain and simple. Although the EU was recognized as a global actor worthy of engagement and even emulation, it was never perceived by Moscow as a neutral entity. Rather, it was seen as the economic counterpart to NATO.

As the negotiations of the Association Agreement neared completion in the late summer of 2011, Moscow began to respond more favourably to Kyiv's long-standing demands for free trade, including a new CIS-wide trade agreement. The economic crisis of 2008–9 had severely impacted Ukraine's economy, making the leadership and oligarchic elites particularly eager to eliminate the recurring and arbitrary trade and customs restrictions imposed by Russia. They sought a legal framework that would constrain Russia's use of ad hoc protectionist measures. Although Russia had frequently promised free trade in its dealings with Ukraine and other CIS partners, it consistently resisted binding commitments, preferring vague and general frameworks (Dragneva and de Kort, 2007). Seeking to leverage its influence, Moscow shifted its position in October 2011 and agreed to sign the draft free trade agreement that had been circulating since the beginning of the year, hoping to stall Ukraine's European integration in the process.

The focus of this new CIS-wide FTA was exclusively on trade issues, a feature that suited Ukraine well. Kyiv could continue its integration with the EU, as the CIS FTA was deemed compatible with the EU's DCFTA (Dragneva and Wolczuk, 2015a). The fact that Kyiv initialled the DCFTA before ratifying the CIS FTA testifies to the latter's importance to the Ukrainian elite. However, from the Russian perspective, the primary purpose of a CIS FTA was not trade liberalization. It formed part of the broader strategy to draw Ukraine into the Customs Union.

In a familiar pattern, any concessions offered by Russia were minimal and accompanied by conditions that ultimately constrained Kyiv's policy options. In particular, the final draft of the CIS agreement included a last-minute but pivotal annex. This provision granted Customs Union member states the unilateral right to revoke trade preferences if a signatory concluded an agreement with a third party that caused, or posed a risk of causing, harm to the Customs Union. The clause lacked clarity regarding the criteria and procedures for its application, yet it clearly established a mechanism through which Russia could penalize Ukraine for signing the Association Agreement with the EU.

Faced with public backlash over this clause, some Ukrainian officials attempted to downplay its significance, assuring the public that 'nothing will change … it is a virtual contract as before' (Shapovalov, 2012). However, the utility of this provision to Russia's interests soon became evident, as subsequent developments demonstrate.

Throughout most of 2012, the prospect of Ukraine signing the Association Agreement with the EU remained uncertain, largely due to the EU's objections to Kyiv's practices of selective justice. However, by spring 2013, both sides began to show signs of flexibility. Attempting to navigate a middle path, President Yanukovych signed a Memorandum of Understanding between Ukraine and the Eurasian Economic Commission in May 2013. The Memorandum provided for non-voting participation in the meetings of the integration bodies of the Customs Union and promised Ukraine's status of an observer in the future Eurasian Economic Union. Nevertheless, this gesture failed to satisfy the Kremlin, which remained deeply frustrated by Ukraine's tendency to give vague undertakings.

In 2013, Moscow launched a renewed offensive, both rhetorical and economic, against the EU–Ukraine Association Agreement. This included a fresh wave of trade restrictions, notably intensified customs checks that effectively halted Ukrainian exports to Russia during the summer of 2013, causing significant damage to Ukrainian businesses. Yet, rather than deterring Ukraine, this pressure appeared to reinforce Yanukovych's resolve to proceed with the signing of the agreement.

However, by late 2013, the cumulative impact of Russia's coercive tactics began to take its toll on Ukraine. The country slid into recession, and the looming threat of economic default altered Yanukovych's political calculus. Although he remained committed to signing the agreement as late as early autumn – when preparations were under way for the Eastern Partnership summit in Vilnius in November – Moscow seized the opportunity to offer substantial economic support in exchange for Ukraine's withdrawal from the agreement.

This offer was flanked by repeated and explicit threats, including the possibility of Russian occupation of Crimea and parts of south-eastern Ukraine (Plokhy, 2023). The deal was negotiated at the highest political level, bypassing conventional diplomatic and governmental channels, during a series of secret meetings between Yanukovych and Putin in October and November 2013. Final details were concluded in Moscow in December.

In essence, Moscow nominally achieved only the 'postponement' of the signing of the agreement with the EU. However, this merely served to camouflage a decisive U-turn. For the very first time, Ukraine prioritized relations with Moscow over integration with the EU. By sabotaging 'association' with the EU, Moscow avoided Ukraine's exit from Russia's realm. There is no definitive evidence that Yanukovych actually committed to Ukraine's accession to the

Eurasian Economic Union, yet such a commitment appears highly plausible (Dragneva and Wolczuk, 2015a).

Moreover, Russia significantly increased its leverage over Ukraine by offering a $15 billion financial loan, a 40 per cent reduction in gas prices, and the familiar promise of trade 'normalization'. This time, however, these incentives came with stringent conditions.[12] Yanukovych was placed on a short leash, effectively limiting his ability to engage in future strategic manoeuvring with Moscow. The Kremlin had learned its lesson: having invested heavily in the Eurasian integration project, it was now intent on fully exploiting Ukraine's economic dependence to secure its participation.

Yet, Yanukovych's readiness to mortgage Ukraine's 'European choice' to Russia in pursuit of his political survival provoked mass protests in Kyiv. Euromaidan Square became the epicentre of the Revolution of Dignity, and the resulting popular resistance led to the collapse of Yanukovych's regime (Wilson, 2015; Onuch and Sasse, 2016; Popova and Shevel, 2023). With Yanukovych fleeing to Russia, Putin was once again confronted with a spectacular and humiliating failure to bind Ukraine to a Russia-led union.

Nevertheless, even after the Euromaidan backlash, Russia had not entirely abandoned its efforts to halt Ukraine's reorientation toward the EU. Confronted with Ukraine's continued defiance, Moscow relied on the EU to make its relations with Ukraine conditional upon Moscow's consent. In a final attempt to restrict Ukraine's economic alignment with the EU, the Kremlin pushed for revisions to the Association Agreement through trilateral negotiations involving the

[12] The $15 billion loan was to be disbursed in instalments, enabling Russia to introduce additional conditionality for each instalment. The lowering of gas prices was discretionary, to be reviewed quarterly. Furthermore, the package of agreements testified to the interest of Russian business in the 'co-ownership and co-management of key sectors of Ukraine's economy' (Onyshkiv, 2013).

EU, Ukraine and Russia, or at the very least, to delay its implementation (Dragneva and Wolczuk, 2015a). These trilateral talks made clear that Russia's claims of economic harm were largely unfounded. Nonetheless, they provided Moscow with a platform to articulate its perceived entitlement over Ukraine. Russia invoked the supposed 'precedence' of its links with Ukraine – regardless of the limited and selective legal commitments Ukraine had made to Russia – over any agreements with the EU.

In these negotiations, Moscow went so far as to claim the right to represent and safeguard what it considered to be Ukraine's best interests (Dragneva and Wolczuk, 2015a). In a distinctly patrimonial fashion, Russia positioned itself as the sole guarantor of Ukraine's 'true' sovereignty. Its objections to the incompatibility of integration regimes revealed a broader attempt to delineate and defend its patrimony, effectively denying the sovereign right of Ukraine to leave it by closer integration with the EU. Russia's efforts to sabotage the Association Agreement failed and the DCFTA began its provisional application in January 2016. In response, Moscow suspended the application of the CIS FTA to Ukraine and imposed Most-Favoured Nation tariffs. The Kremlin anticipated that this would trigger an economic collapse in Ukraine, prompting it to turn back to Russia (Trenin, 2014), a scenario that did not materialize.

Conclusions

For nearly three decades, Moscow had sought to reintegrate Ukraine into a Russia-led union. Throughout this period, Ukraine's leadership consistently exercised caution in its engagements with Russia (see Table 6.1). Thus, Kyiv avoided any open-ended, comprehensive, legally binding commitment to 'deeper' forms of economic integration, such as economic unions. Instead, Kyiv preferred to pursue targeted solutions to immediate economic challenges, such as free trade agreements.

Despite concerns over sovereignty, however, Ukraine made itself vulnerable to Moscow's overtures, and Russia was able to harness Ukraine's economic dependence to secure its vision of the post-Soviet 'space'. The more vulnerable Kyiv became – at times of economic hardship or electoral uncertainty, when the political survival of ruling elites was at stake – the more likely it was to align with Russia's preferences.

Unsurprisingly, Russia's strategy relied on high-level, opaque and ad hoc negotiations, shaped by Moscow's evolving integration agenda and the short-term political and economic interests of Ukraine's elites. Treaty drafting was routinely accompanied by intensive political campaigning and economic pressure.

Even when Moscow failed to secure Ukraine's membership in a new union, it remained intent on obstructing Ukraine's pro-European trajectory. The political backlash in Ukraine, including the Revolution of Dignity and the subsequent reaffirmation of Ukraine's European course, once again dashed Moscow's hopes.

Against this background, Russia's resort to military force was not merely a reaction to the ousting of Yanukovych; it was, above all, an expression of long-standing frustration with Kyiv's persistent refusal to reintegrate with Russia, despite repeated overtures and persistent economic dependence. Ironically, the use of military force disrupted the complex patterns of interdependence that had characterized the relationship for decades. In its effort to preserve sovereignty, Ukraine incurred previously unimaginable costs – including the curtailment of its trade and energy ties with Russia – as will be explored in the next chapter.

SEVEN

Cutting Ukraine Down to Size (2014–21)

Until early 2014, Russia nominally respected Ukraine's statehood while simultaneously ensuring it remained within its patrimony through the deployment of the political and economic tools at its disposal. Concurrently, Moscow's efforts to restore Ukraine to its 'natural state' of formal unity with Russia persisted, gaining new urgency following Putin's ascent to power in 2000 (see Chapter 6). Between 1991 and 2014, however, Kyiv consistently resisted Russia's attempts to secure Ukraine's full membership in its integration projects, opting instead for a minimal and selective level of commitment. This persistent reluctance underscored the failure of Russia's efforts to achieve its aims via 'skilful diplomacy': Ukraine proved more resistant to the Kremlin's manoeuvring than anticipated in 1991. Nevertheless, Ukraine's half-hearted but repeated engagement with Russian integration ventures fostered a false perception in Moscow that, with sufficient pressure, Ukraine would eventually commit unequivocally to a Russia-led union, a strategy that had proven highly effective in Belarus.

The limitations of this approach were starkly revealed during the *Maidan* protests in the winter of 2013–14. The dramatic collapse of Yanukovych's regime under the weight of immense civil protest derailed Russia's reintegration plans and revitalized Kyiv's relations with the EU. In Moscow, this shift was interpreted as a breach of an unwritten – but presumed self-evident – understanding of Ukraine's limited sovereignty and Russia's prerogative to determine its governance, including the parameters of its cooperation with the West. This was not only about Ukraine's historical attachment to Russia, but – given Russia's patrimonial conception of sovereignty – also about a perceived encroachment upon Russia itself.

In response, in 2014 Moscow abandoned its nominal respect for Ukraine's territorial integrity and borders, seeking instead to redefine the very terms of Ukraine's statehood. First, it challenged the legitimacy of Ukraine's post-Maidan government, styling itself as the defender of the 'true will' of the people. Second, it unilaterally revised Ukraine's borders through the occupation of Crimea. Third, Moscow set out to reshape Ukraine's constitutional and territorial structure by using regional proxies as leverage over the central government in Kyiv. The Kremlin orchestrated separatist movements in Eastern Ukraine, through both covert and overt military actions, and insisted that Ukraine reintegrate these regions under revised constitutional arrangements. This signalled a fundamental departure from the post-Soviet etiquette of relations between sovereign states. Moscow now sought to dismantle Ukraine's sovereignty (Barbieri, 2025). However, Russia's campaign remained cloaked in international law rhetoric, stretching legal interpretations to suit its needs and, crucially, to secure Western acquiescence. This chapter examines these developments in detail to show the Kremlin's strategy and its ultimate failure.[1]

Delegitimizing Ukraine's government

For Moscow, the etiquette of Ukraine's sovereignty was acceptable only insofar as it de facto remained under Russia's patrimonial control. This system depended on securing the

[1] This chapter builds on sections of Chapter 7 in Dragneva and Wolczuk (2015a).

loyalty of political elites in Ukraine in order to ensure that Russian interests consistently prevailed. Such an approach was most effective in an environment of opaque governance and the suppression of opposition; conditions that characterized President Yanukovych's government until the eruption of the Maidan protests.

In response to the regime's collapse in early 2014, Moscow framed the post-Maidan government as a result of the 'coup' that violated Ukraine's constitutional order. The coup narrative served to formally absolve the Kremlin of its prior commitments to respect Ukraine's sovereignty, thereby legitimizing its subsequent actions to revise Ukraine's borders. In an interview on 4 March 2014, Putin likened the events to the fall of the Russian Empire in 1917. Rather confusingly, he argued it had led to the emergence of a new state, one 'with which we have signed no binding agreements'.[2] Russia portrayed the new Ukrainian government as unrepresentative and asserted its right to defend the interests of the Ukrainian people who, it claimed, had been betrayed by their own leadership. These interests, according to Moscow, were best served through renewed union with Russia. Echoing Soviet-era practices, the Kremlin assumed the role of arbiter in determining the legitimacy and suitability of the governments of its satellite states.[3] Implicit in this stance was the deeply held belief of Russia's elites that Ukraine's statehood was inherently unsustainable outside the Russian world.

In practice, however, the situation was more nuanced. The Kremlin did not repudiate all of Russia's previous agreements

2 'Vladimir Putin answered journalists' questions on the situation in Ukraine', 4 March 2014, http://en.kremlin.ru/events/president/news/20366.

3 As Kennan summed up the Soviet approach, 'Moscow established itself as the arbiter as to which foreign factions, in power or out of it, were deserving of popular support – which foreign governments may be tolerated, and which should be opposed and overthrown' (1961: 189).

with Kyiv; rather, it adopted a highly selective approach. For instance, it denounced the 1997 BSF Accords, which were deemed obsolete following Crimea's 'return to Russia'. Yet, it refrained from denouncing the 1997 Treaty of Friendship, which promoted unity through 'partnership and cooperation'.[4] To intensify pressure on Ukraine, Moscow upheld the 2009 energy deal, unfavourable to Kyiv, while disregarding the 2010 Kharkiv Accord, which offered Ukraine a beneficial energy discount. Similarly, Russia continued to recognize certain provisions of the 2003 Agreement on the Use of the Azov Sea and the Kerch Strait, while declaring others void (see Chapter 5).

Ultimately, Putin asserted that, due to the alleged 'coup', Moscow no longer had 'a partner at the top level' in Ukraine.[5] Nevertheless, by calling for new presidential and parliamentary elections in Kyiv, Moscow signalled its continued ambition to manage Ukraine and bring it back into the fold by other means.

Return to conquest by force

Despite Moscow's long-standing challenges to the legality of Crimea's transfer to Ukraine and its efforts to foment Crimean separatism during the 1990s, it ultimately agreed to respect Ukraine's *de jure* territorial integrity (see Chapter 4). This adherence to the etiquette of international law governing the relations between two nominally sovereign states came to an abrupt end with the occupation of Crimea in 2014, legal formalities notwithstanding (Wilson, 2015; Plokhy, 2023).

The land grab was facilitated by the collapse of President Yanukovych's regime, which created the space for Moscow to act, while the new government asserted control. At that

4 The 1997 Friendship Treaty eventually expired in 2018.

5 'Vladimir Putin answered journalists' questions on the situation in Ukraine', 4 March 2014.

moment, Kyiv had yet to reassert full control over its armed forces and security apparatus. Seizing the opportunity, Moscow launched its military assault to occupy the peninsula on 27 February 2014, an action that bore all the hallmarks of a planned operation (Darczewska, 2014). Putin initially denied involvement, only to retract this denial.[6] In flagrant violation of the Black Sea Fleet Accords, Russian troops stationed at the Sevastopol naval base were deployed to take control of key infrastructure across Crimea (Weller, 2022). As Ukraine followed Western counsel to desist from fighting back to avoid military escalation, Russian forces encountered minimal resistance (Plokhy, 2023).

Simultaneously, unmarked Russian forces seized control of Crimea's legitimate public authorities, threatening the Crimean parliament into submission and installing a new de facto head of government.[7] In a move reminiscent of Soviet-era performative legality, a referendum on the status of Crimea was hastily staged on 16 March 2014. The ballot presented two options: first, the restoration of the 1992 Crimean Constitution, granting expanded increased powers to the Crimean parliament relative to Ukraine's central government, or, second, joining Russia as a subject of the Russian Federation. Neither option was clearly defined,[8] yet both implied the peninsula's de facto separation from Ukraine. Crucially, the referendum excluded the possibility of maintaining the status quo, which Moscow had already dismissed.

---

6 See Putin's testimony in the documentary 'Crimea. The Road to the Motherland', available at: www.youtube.com/watch?v=t42-71RpRgI.

7 Sergei Aksenov, who became the new prime minister, headed the Russian Unity Party, sponsored by the Russian security services, which had received only 4 per cent of the vote at Crimean parliamentary elections (Plokhy, 2023: 112).

8 For example, as explained in Chapter 4, the use of 'sovereignty' at the time was legally ambiguous, not to mention the fact that the Crimean Constitution underwent significant changes over the course of 1992.

The results were announced the following day and swiftly followed by the Crimean parliament's proclamation of independence and formal request to join Russia. Moscow immediately recognized Crimea as a sovereign state and proceeded with another legal rubber stamp: a Treaty on the Accession of the Republic of Crimea to the Russian Federation on 20 March, which was ratified by the Russian Federal Assembly on 21 March 2014. Ironically, upon accession, Crimea was designated as a mere federal district within the Russian Federation, thereby forfeiting the autonomous status it had held within Ukraine from 1991 to 2014, an autonomy Russia had previously insisted upon.[9] Conquest and amalgamation were back.

Despite the UN General Assembly's resolution declaring the referendum invalid and, thus, incapable of altering Crimea's legal status,[10] Moscow asserted the legality of its actions. It advanced an array of justifications – manufacturing the facts where needed – to fit various international law principles, including self-determination, intervention by invitation, and the responsibility to protect Russian citizens from danger. These wide-ranging legal justifications were interwoven with ethno-historical references and appeals to historical justice, producing what Allison (2014: 1259) aptly describes as 'justificatory smokescreens' that blurred the boundaries between legality and illegality. Moscow's approach amounted to a 'strategy of legal ambiguity', invoking concepts without fully articulating them; offering hypothetical justifications for actions it had initially denied, only to acknowledge them later on (Marxen, 2016: 13). These arguments were widely discredited by the international legal community (Allison, 2014, 2020; Geiss, 2015; Grant,

9 In 2016, the Crimean federal district was subsumed under the Southern federal district.

10 UNGA Resolution 68/272 'Territorial Integrity of Ukraine', 27 March 2014. The resolution was preceded by a draft resolution brought before the Security Council, which Russia vetoed.

2015; Marxen, 2016; Pursiainen and Forsberg, 2018; Dubinsky and Rutland, 2019; Weller, 2022). Nonetheless, Russia's tactics proved effective in cultivating 'plausible deniability' (Allison, 2014), which tempered international responses to the annexation. Many observers swiftly accepted Russia's tenuous historical claim to Crimea (Darczewska, 2014; Kuzio, 2020; Finnin, 2022), treating the annexation as a singular event and therefore, a fait accompli, that would eventually be followed by the gradual normalization of relations with Moscow.

The Crimean occupation proved to be only the opening salvo in a broader campaign. Crimea became a staging post for expanding Russia's control over the Azov Sea and the Black Sea and for exerting sustained pressure on Ukraine through military skirmishes and economic strangulation (see Chapter 5). This strategy was designed not only to destabilize and delegitimize the Ukrainian government but also to signal to Western capitals that Ukraine was a failed state, thereby encouraging tacit acceptance of its subjugation (Allan, 2020). More broadly, the occupation served as a stark warning of the consequences of disloyalty to Moscow. Ukraine was effectively 'cut down to size' for defying Moscow and rejecting reintegration with Russia.[11] It was indicative that Russia also hinted at the possibility of reversing its previous recognition of the sovereignty of the Baltic states (Grigas, 2015). Through its demonstrative punishment of Ukraine, Moscow sent a clear message to other post-Soviet states: comply or face the consequences.

De-sovereignizing Ukraine

Although Crimea was presented as an exceptional case, Russia remained fundamentally unwilling to accept the existence of

[11] This was clearly understood by both Belarus and Kazakhstan, who sought to alter their positions in the ongoing negotiations of the Eurasian Economic Union (Dragneva, 2018).

an independent Ukraine. However, it lost important levers over Ukraine in the process. The occupation significantly diminished Moscow's toolbox: millions of pro-Russian voters were removed from Ukraine's electorate, and the broader Ukrainian population became increasingly alienated. More critically, the military intervention failed to deter Kyiv. On the contrary, Ukraine intensified its efforts to align with the EU, as evidenced by the signing of the Association Agreement in March 2014 (Dragneva and Wolczuk, 2015a). Moscow faced a choice: accept the shift in Ukraine's direction or escalate its efforts to reverse it. It chose the latter.

Thus, in March 2014, Russia demanded a fundamental restructuring of the Ukrainian state. The Russian Ministry of Foreign Affairs proposed that Ukraine became a federal state, ostensibly to accommodate its regional differences. As Foreign Minister Lavrov argued, 'Ukraine's western, eastern and southern regions have different political traditions and different interests, and to make Ukraine function as one state, a compromise between all these interests should be found' (Voice of Russia, 2014). In practice, the plan aimed to render Ukraine 'a virtually ungovernable state open to Russian manipulation' (Plokhy, 2023: 121).

In mid-April 2014, Russia revived a long-dormant idea: 'Novorossya', the 19th-century province of the Russian Empire that encompassed the entire east and south of Ukraine. This ad hoc resurrection was an overt attempt to reclaim the possessions of imperial Russia. This was to be achieved by fomenting separatism and providing military support to local proxies, all while framing the unrest as an indigenous rebellion against Kyiv (Allan, 2020; Plokhy, 2023). This project was put into practice when unmarked Russian special forces, in coordination with local militants, seized administrative and police buildings across cities and towns in eastern and southern Ukraine. The campaign of orchestrated violence was reinforced by the threat of direct Russian military intervention under the guise of a 'peacekeeping' mission, should Ukraine attempt a counter-offensive.[12] Simultaneously, Moscow launched an intensive political and media campaign to agitate the local population across south-eastern Ukraine against the new Kyiv authorities. Despite these efforts, the concept of Novorossya failed to gain traction among the population, resulting in only limited unrest in cities such as Kharkiv and Odessa during April and May 2014.

Consequently, the Kremlin concentrated its efforts on the Donbas. Its strategy amounted to 'armed suasion', that is 'the limited use of force and other tools of pressure by one external state against a target state', in order to influence the latter, but without engaging in sustained warfare (Lynch, 2000: 4). The objective of this approach was twofold: first, to establish Russian-controlled enclaves, and second, to compel Ukraine to reintegrate these territories on political terms dictated by Moscow.

Armed suasion in the Donbas

Once a 'showcase of communism', the Donbas region fell into decline post-independence, experiencing widespread poverty, economic stagnation and a growing sense of marginalization and resentment. These conditions created fertile ground for exploitation by the local elites and Russian commanders (Wilson, 2015). Russia's orchestrated armed rebellion succeeded in igniting conflict in parts of the Donbas region, specifically within the Donetsk and Luhansk *oblasts*.

The insurgency was initiated by Kremlin operatives, armed by the Russian military, manned predominantly by Russian fighters, and directed from Moscow. It resulted in the proclamation of the Donetsk People's Republic (DPR) and the Luhansk People's Republic (LPR) in April 2014.

[12] Some 40,000 Russian troops were kept in position, on occasion engaging in exercises to demonstrate that they were ready to cross the border.

Sham referenda were held in both regions on 11 May 2014, after which their 'statehood' was declared. Although de facto leaders of DPR and LPR pleaded for accession to Russia, this contradicted Moscow's plans. At this stage, Russia did not seek formal recognition of the DPR and LPR as separate states; rather, these entities were intended to serve as constitutional levers to exert pressure on Kyiv.[13] To implement this plan, Moscow consolidated control over the two regions during the summer of 2014, systematically purging activists who promoted alternative strategies (Allan, 2020).

However, unlike in Crimea, Ukraine mounted a military response to Russia's intervention, launching an 'Anti-Terrorist Operation' that led to intense clashes between the Ukrainian and the Russian forces. The successful Ukrainian counter-offensive in the early summer of 2014 prompted Russia to escalate its involvement, including artillery attacks launched from Russian territory. By August 2014, the presence of regular Russian military troops on Ukrainian soil had become permanent.

As hostilities intensified in the summer of 2014, including the massacre of Ukrainian troops by Russian forces in Ilovaisk, international pressure mounted to secure a ceasefire. France and Germany spearheaded the creation of the 'Normandy format', which established a trilateral contact group comprising Ukraine, Russia and the OSCE to pursue diplomatic resolution. These efforts led to the negotiation of a ceasefire protocol in Minsk on 5 September 2014 (the so-called 'Minsk-1'). However, the deal soon broke down, with Moscow escalating its military operations over the winter of 2014–15. In January 2015, heavy fighting involving Russian regular troops and armoured units, resulted in further territorial gains and the encirclement of

[13] Russia recognized the statehood of both entities only on 21 February 2022 as part of the package of measures at the launch of its full-scale invasion of Ukraine.

Ukrainian troops near Debaltseve.[14] This prompted a renewed Franco-German diplomatic initiative, culminating in a summit in Minsk in February 2015. After a gruelling negotiating marathon, on 12 February 2015 Russia secured an additional protocol to the ceasefire agreement ('Minsk-2'), containing a 'package of measures' to achieve a new peace settlement.

This 'package of measures' covered four main areas, summarized by Dumoulin (2024) as follows:

1. Security: the establishment of a ceasefire, monitored by a special OSCE mission; the withdrawal of forces and heavy weapons on both sides of the line of contact; the disarmament of illegal groups; and the withdrawal of foreign fighters.
2. Humanitarian aspects: the exchange of prisoners and provisions regarding humanitarian access (with de-mining added later).
3. Economy: at first, the drafting of an economic development plan for Donbas; and after the end of hostilities, a dialogue on the resumption of economic relations across the line of contact.
4. Political issues: the status of the Donetsk and Luhansk regions, with Ukraine to introduce a constitutional reform including a law on self-government for these regions; the holding of local elections in these regions; and an amnesty for participants from the Donetsk and Luhansk regions.

The provisions of Minsk-2 were vague and sketchy, poorly drafted, and open to interpretation. Greater clarity regarding Moscow's intentions emerged not from the text itself, but through Russia's unilateral reinterpretation of its terms over the

[14] By March 2015, there were 10,500–11,000 Russian troops operating in eastern Ukraine (Sutyagin, 2015).

subsequent eight years. Despite being hailed as the blueprint out of the crisis, the Minsk-2 'peace plan' was in fact a façade, concealing Russia's underlying objective of reconfiguring Ukraine's statehood in line with its interests. This veneer was sustained by Moscow's portrayal of itself as a neutral actor and was accepted by a credulous West. Despite substantial evidence of Russia's direct involvement, including the presence of Russian troops and weaponry on Ukrainian territory, Western governments, media and segments of academia repeatedly downplayed Moscow's direct involvement. Russia consistently denied being a party to the conflict, and the West largely acquiesced to this fiction.

More specifically, Moscow presented itself as a neutral mediator seeking to pacify what it characterized as a civil war; an internal conflict allegedly sparked by local unrest. This framing was crucial in shaping the legal definition of the conflict, particularly in determining 'the source or paradigm of applicable law and any consequent action to identify and assign legal responsibilities and demand accountability' (Bachmann and Mosquera, 2015: 28). To reinforce this narrative, Russia ensured that representatives of the DPR and LPR participated in the negotiations with Ukraine, and formally signed the Minsk-2 agreement, while Russia positioned itself as a peace broker and international guarantor. This manoeuvre enabled Moscow to embed its political demands within the ceasefire and peace deal, effectively pausing its aggression without acknowledging responsibility or incurring legal accountability for its own use of force. As Dumoulin (2024) observes, none of the provisions in the agreements explicitly imposed any obligations on Moscow.

At the same time, the imperative of peace-making enabled Russia to draw on international actors in service of its aims. This marked a departure from its previous approach of seeking to keep the EU, and international actors in general, out of its regional affairs, particularly in relation to Ukraine. Thus, Russia now sought to co-opt select EU member states, evoking the record of historical European alliances, to exert pressure on Ukraine to accept a peace plan.

Within the Normandy format, the involvement of Germany and France – despite their limited strategic interest in Ukraine – played into Moscow's agenda. Reluctant to confront Russia directly, the leaders of both countries acquiesced to its demands and embraced the Minsk agreements as the only viable path forward. In doing so, they effectively submitted to Russia's strategy of armed suasion, motivated by the desire to avert what President Putin described as the risk of Ukraine 'being crashed'. Their role became instrumental in delivering a deal that was marked by the kind of ambiguity typical of urgent diplomatic solutions to crises that had not been fully understood – let alone confronted – by the intermediating parties (Allan, 2020). This acquiescence was most evident in the way the deal was reached: a gruelling marathon of negotiations designed to physically exhaust the Ukrainian, German and French leaders. It was further reflected in the agreement's poor drafting, which left ample room for ambiguity and incompatible interpretations regarding both the substance and sequencing of its implementation.

Federalisation à la Minsk

Ukraine's acute sense of vulnerability in the face of an increasingly belligerent Russia made the restoration of its sovereignty within internationally recognized borders a paramount priority. This imperative placed all options on the table, including openness to decentralization, enhanced powers for local authorities, and the possibility of early local elections. These elements were reflected in the 2014 peace plan proposed by Ukraine's newly elected president, Petro Poroshenko (2014–19), which also included the creation of a buffer zone and a safe corridor to facilitate the withdrawal of insurgents from Ukrainian territory (Shandra, 2019). Bearing the hallmarks of sovereign decision-making, the plan envisioned a return to constitutional normalcy through the removal of unlawful armed formations and the reassertion of Ukrainian control over its borders (Allan, 2020). In contrast to externally driven frameworks, Poroshenko's initiative represented a nationally determined effort to restore order and uphold Ukraine's territorial integrity.

Yet this was decidedly not the outcome Russia sought from the negotiation process. In the Minsk-1 agreement, Moscow succeeded in pressuring Kyiv to commit to passing legislation on the temporary special status of DPR and LPR and hold local elections under it as the price for the cessation of hostilities. By February 2015 when Minsk-2 was signed, Moscow escalated its demands, pushing for constitutional reform, including a permanent law on the special status of these entities and the adoption of a new constitution by the end of the same year. Contrary to interpretations that viewed these provisions as merely 'approximating a modicum of local self-governance' (Weller, 2022: 7), they represented a direct challenge to Ukraine's statehood in several significant respects. The measures proposed by Moscow were not aimed at decentralization in the conventional sense, but rather at embedding Russian influence within Ukraine's constitutional framework, thereby undermining its sovereignty.

First, the Minsk-2 agreement provided broad and open-ended parameters for the 'special status' of the two enclaves.[15] This constituted a direct encroachment on Ukraine's sovereign right to freely determine its own constitutional order (Hedenskog, 2014). Shortly thereafter, Moscow expanded its demands to include the right of these regions to conclude agreements with foreign states, financial autonomy and, most

[15] For example, Minsk-2 listed the need for 'agreements with the relevant local authorities on economic, social and cultural development' and 'assistance for the central government to cross-border cooperation' between Donetsk and Luhansk and regions of the Russian Federation.

significantly, the inclusion of a neutrality clause in Ukraine's constitution (Shandra, 2019). The implementation of such political terms would have amounted to the insertion of 'a constitutional Trojan horse that would give the Kremlin a lasting presence in Ukraine's political system' (Allan, 2020: 13). This is because such arrangements would have severely constrained Ukraine's ability to govern independently, effectively giving Russia a veto over key policy areas, including foreign and security policy, and undermining its aspirations for NATO and EU membership, thereby institutionalizing Ukraine's limited sovereignty.

Second, the threat to Ukraine's security remained unresolved. In the process of implementing Minsk-2, President Poroshenko insisted on prioritizing the security agenda as a precondition for any political settlement in the Donbas, encapsulated in the notion of 'no elections without security guarantees'. In contrast, Russia made constitutional reform a precondition for restoring Kyiv's control over its borders. As a result, no meaningful ceasefire, disarmament or withdrawal of Russian-backed militants was to occur until Moscow had secured its political wins: this was an extension of its armed suasion tactic. This sequencing trap in Minsk-2 proved deeply problematic (Kostanyan and Meister, 2016; Atland, 2020). The prescribed sequencing rendered key obligations, such as holding elections in Donbas in accordance with OSCE standards, virtually impossible to fulfil (Allan, 2020). Crucially, it created a unique legal situation in which Ukraine's sovereignty was implicitly conditioned on compliance with the Minsk agreements (Tzimas, 2024). On balance, the consequences of implementing the deal on Russia's terms would have been devastating for Ukraine's statehood.[16] In parallel, Russia sought to discredit Ukraine internationally,

[16] Despite being heralded as 'agreements', the protocols were little more than lists of badly drafted points, whose legal nature was problematic. For example, they were not signed by heads of state or foreign ministers,

pointing to its alleged failure to implement the terms of the deal.

Third, as Ukraine faced intense military pressure, the deal imposed disproportionately greater obligations on Ukraine than on the separatist forces (Kardaś and Konończuk, 2015; Silina, 2015; Meister, 2015). Simultaneously, the accords operated within a legal vacuum, detached from the broader context of Ukraine's bilateral relations with Russia. Notably, the absence of any reference to Crimea signalled a tacit acceptance of its occupation. Furthermore, the agreements failed to acknowledge prior treaties between Russia and Ukraine or any pertinent international legal frameworks, thereby implicitly endorsing Moscow's attempt to nullify its previous commitments to respect Ukraine's sovereignty, territorial integrity and borders.

In sum, Russia employed a combination of military and diplomatic instruments to coerce Ukraine to enact its political demands. Central to Moscow's strategy was reconfiguring Ukraine as a federation: through the use of pro-Russian regions as proxies, it attempted to achieve de facto control over the Donbas, while maintaining the region's status as *de jure* part of Ukraine. Moscow's covert measures ensured the acquiescence of the West and plausible denial of Russian actions. Ignoring its fundamental contradictions, both the US and EU accepted Minsk-2 as a 'baseline', putting pressure on Ukraine to implement it. Instead of breaking the deadlock, the plans of international interlocutors, such as the German Foreign Minister Steinmeier, effectively reinforced Russia's preferences and permitted Moscow to make further negotiations contingent upon Ukraine's implementation of the accords (Atland, 2020).

nor did they follow set treaty-making procedures, even though they were subsequently endorsed by a UN Security Council resolution 2202 (2015) (Atland, 2020). There were questions as to the effects of the signatures of the unelected leaders of the two self-proclaimed republics (Tzimas, 2024).

The limits of armed suasion

Through the creation of separatist entities and Minsk-2, Moscow succeeded in securing international legitimacy for its actions and expanded its capacity to exert pressure on Kyiv. However, this strategy was both complex and fraught with risk (Barbieri, 2025). It depended on Ukraine's willingness to implement Russian demands precisely at a moment when those demands, and Russia's broader objectives, were clearly comprehended in Kyiv. As Barbieri (2025) points out, the DPR and LPR were rapidly integrated into the Russian political, economic and legal systems, leaving little ambiguity regarding Moscow's intentions for the rest of Ukraine. Despite sustained economic, military and diplomatic pressure, Ukraine was able to at least partially thwart Russian plans.

A pivotal aspect of this resistance concerned the implementation of Russia's demands in Minsk-2. Adhering to the principle of 'security before status', Ukraine stipulated that elections in the occupied territories would only be held once militia and foreign military formations had withdrawn and Ukraine had regained control over its borders in the Donbas. Moreover, the proposal to grant permanent 'special status' to the DPR and LPR encountered significant domestic opposition. In August 2015, violent clashes erupted during a parliamentary debate over constitutional amendments proposed by President Poroshenko, which would have granted enhanced self-government to the Donetsk and Luhansk regions. No further attempts to pass through such amendments were made and Poroshenko's draft law was formally withdrawn in 2019 (Shandra, 2019). While Ukraine implemented decentralization by strengthening local self-government, federalization remained firmly off the agenda. Concurrently, in response to the de facto integration of DPR and LPR with Russia, Ukraine refused to support the economies of the occupied regions. Kyiv initiated an economic blockade of the Donbas, effectively severing the separatist regions from Ukraine's markets and financial systems (Barbieri, 2025).

In parallel, Kyiv took steps to de-couple Ukraine from Russia, thereby limiting Moscow's ability to exert pressure across multiple domains. One significant step was the assertion of religious independence through the recognition of the autocephalous Ukrainian Orthodox Church (Sherr and Kullamaa, 2019). The *tomos* of autocephaly, issued by the Patriarch of Constantinople in January 2019, marked a substantial victory for Ukraine in challenging the Kremlin's claims to historical and religious unity (Liik et al, 2019; Hurak and D'Anieri, 2022).

Ukraine also moved to further reduce its economic dependence on Russia. In retaliation for Ukraine's progress toward signing the trade part of the Association Agreement with the EU, Moscow unilaterally ceased applying the CIS FTA and imposed Most-Favoured Nation tariffs on Ukrainian goods as of January 2016 (see Chapter 6). This compelled Ukraine to undertake a radical reorientation of its trade toward the EU and other global markets, despite the considerable economic costs involved.[17]

Finally, Kyiv also took the pivotal step of reducing its energy dependence on Russia. In 2014, the new Ukrainian government challenged the pricing formula embedded in the 2009 gas contract and sought renegotiation. Russia refused and, consistent with its selective approach to legality, revoked the discount granted under the 2010 Kharkiv Accords. As negotiations collapsed, Russia suspended gas supplies, forcing Ukraine to rely on limited domestic extraction and reverse flows of cheaper Russian gas from Poland, Hungary and Slovakia. As a result, for the first time in its post-Soviet history, Ukraine ceased importing gas directly from Russia (Wolczuk, 2016).

[17] The value of Ukraine's imports to Russia decreased threefold between 2014 and 2015 – from $12 billion to $4 billion. By the autumn of 2015, Russia's share in Ukraine's trade fell to 18 per cent (Wolczuk, 2016).

Overall, in the face of military aggression, Ukraine demonstrated a willingness to absorb the costs of diminished trade and energy ties with Russia. In other words, Russia's use of force disrupted the complex and long-standing patterns of dependence that had previously enabled it to steer Ukraine into a union with Russia. In this context, Minsk-2 appears to have marked a watershed in Russian-Ukrainian relations: it precipitated the end of Ukraine's political, economic and energy dependence on Russia, thereby depriving Moscow of the tools it had used since the very first days of Ukrainian independence to sway Kyiv into submission.

Conclusions

In 2014, Russia reverted to the radical strategy of using military means to secure Ukraine's obedience. Paradoxically, this shift rendered the achievement of its objectives more difficult, if not entirely unattainable. Armed suasion relies on the willingness of the authorities in the target state to comply with demands, yet they are often deemed unacceptable due to their emanation from an aggressor state. Thus, Russia's coercive tactics simultaneously advanced and undermined its political goals, necessitating repeated applications of force and agreements to secure compliance. This cycle of aggression further alienated the Ukrainian population and intensified resistance, as evidenced by the increasingly firm stance of President Poroshenko and, then, his successor, Volodymyr Zelensky.

Elected in 2019 on a platform promising peace with Russia, Zelensky's negotiations over the Minsk-2 agreement during 2019–20 only underscored the risks inherent in accepting Russia's expansive demands. Rather than facilitating resolution, Moscow's belligerence hardened Kyiv's resolve. Consequently, Russia's strategy of armed suasion failed comprehensively: following Minsk-2, Russia found itself further from achieving its objectives in Ukraine than ever before.

Nevertheless, this setback did not persuade Moscow of the futility of its strategy. On the contrary, the failure to achieve its aims, coupled with a diminishing set of tools at its disposal, led Russia to escalate further. Moscow opted for an overt, full-scale invasion, aiming to eliminate Ukraine's capacity for resistance or to deny its right to exist as a country.

EIGHT

From Failure to Failure?

In Russia, the patrimonial model of power shaped the rulers' self-perception and practice as masters and owners of territories and peoples. Historically, the patrimonial rule expanded over new territories: it transcended Russia's formal borders, justifying territorial expansion and permeating its foreign policy. This model underpinned the Russian conception of sovereignty. From Moscow's perspective, only a few states are truly sovereign, a view that has persisted from the tsarist era through the Bolshevik period. The tsars exercised power freely. The Bolsheviks justified expansion and dominance through communism, centralizing authority and suppressing opposition, even when they formally endorsed the right to self-determination. In the 20th century, the Soviet republics and satellite states embodied the modern adaptations of patrimonial control.

The late 1980s saw the Soviet system's collapse and the emergence of an ostensibly 'new' Russia, alongside rising independence movements in the former republics. Unlike in 1917–21, Ukraine achieved independence in 1991, thereby posing an unprecedented challenge to Russia's patrimonial tradition. Ukraine's sovereignty was fundamentally incompatible with Russia's historical self-conception, as the possession of Ukraine had been central to Muscovy's transformation into Russia. Leaders, from Stalin to Putin, asserted the continuity of a 'thousand-year-old state', conflating Russian, imperial and Soviet identities (Solchanyk, 1992; Zubok, 2021). In this narrative, Ukraine was not and could never be a 'real state' as articulated in Putin's 2021 essay (Duben, 2020).[1] Pushed to its extremes, this sentiment depicted Ukrainianness as a 'specific disorder of the mind' (Surkov, 2020).

The sudden dissolution of the USSR temporarily limited Russia's ability to assert patrimonial control. Confronted with the need for international legitimacy, Yeltsin was compelled to pursue an untested path: peaceful and consensual relations with the other former Soviet republics within the framework of international law. Nevertheless, Russia's acceptance of Ukrainian independence in 1991 was not only reluctant, it was provisional, with the aim of reasserting its patrimonial hold in the not too distant future. This chapter spells out our findings about Russia's post-Soviet patrimonial model, emphasizing Moscow's craft of legal manipulation in constructing it. We conclude by assessing the instrumentalization of international law and its implications for the future of the war, Russia and Eastern Europe.

Russia's post-Soviet patrimonial trajectory

Since 1991, as observed by several scholars, (neo)patrimonialism has continued to define Russia's political trajectory (for example, Robinson, 2017; Domanska, 2019; Lynch, 2021; Pierzynski and Jonathan, 2025). This book argues that the patrimonial model has persisted and fundamentally shaped not only Russia's domestic politics, but its foreign policy too, including the attack on Ukraine. This external dimension is vastly underappreciated, largely due to the limited attention paid to how Russia has upgraded its methods by perfecting the instrumental use of international law in the modern era. Since 1991, Russia has been crafting a post-Soviet patrimonial model,

1 'On the historical unity of Russians and Ukrainians', 12 July 2021, http://en.kremlin.ru/events/president/news/66181. The essay is believed to be authored by former Minister of Culture of Russia, Vladimir Medinsky.

characterized by the interplay of two key components: first, the formal observance of the etiquette of sovereignty in line with the fundamental norms of international law, and second, a new tactic to reimpose Russian control under the guise of legality.

The first of these components involved an adherence to nominal legality. The dissolution of the USSR produced 12 legal successors, establishing Russia and Ukraine as independent and equal sovereign entities. Ukraine's statehood was recognized through a series of political declarations and legal agreements with Moscow, with formal caveats concerning the recognition of existing borders removed by 1997. Russian leaders engaged in inter-state diplomacy, observing the ritual of international agreements and legal protocol. In this context, Zubok's assertion (2021) that, from the Russian perspective, Ukraine was filing for divorce without a settlement, does not withstand empirical scrutiny. Moreover, while Moscow made no secret of its desire for the rapid reintegration of post-Soviet states, it consistently framed this ambition as a voluntary project grounded in inter-state relations and respect for the sovereignty of its members.

The second component of Russia's post-Soviet patrimonial model stands in stark contrast to the first. While ostensibly treating Ukraine as its equal, Russia simultaneously sought to circumscribe Ukraine's sovereignty in multiple ways. These included demands for open state borders, the maintenance of a long-term Russian military presence in Crimea, pressure for nuclear disarmament, assertions of a right to protect Russian nationals abroad, and the encouragement of separatist movements. On the international arena, Russia insisted that 'partnership and cooperation' with Moscow should take precedence over Ukraine's other foreign policy preferences and commitments, effectively seeking to control Kyiv's relations with external actors, such as the EU (Chapter 7). With direct political and military control no longer possible in the post-Soviet period, Moscow weaponized the legacies of the USSR to achieve its goals from 1991 onward. This had limited impact.

Successive Ukrainian leaders struggled to reduce the country's economic dependence on Russia, but they consistently refused to compromise on Ukraine's sovereignty. In general, Ukraine's leaders resisted Russian pressures to rejoin a new union, yielding only when under extreme duress, as exemplified by Yanukovych's U-turn in November 2013 (Dragneva and Wolczuk, 2015a). Even when Ukrainian politicians buckled, popular resistance remained steadfast, most notably during the Euromaidan protests.

Having failed to achieve its objectives through 'skilful diplomacy', Moscow shifted to more coercive methods in 2014, beginning with the annexation of Crimea and followed by armed suasion in Donbas, which it portrayed as a civil war. This shift to covert warfare suggested that either Moscow had exhausted its patience or had come to the conclusion that the remaining economic and political tools available to it were insufficient to 'coerce Ukraine into friendship' (Sherr and Gretskiy, 2023). Nevertheless, Moscow remained hopeful that

> economic hardships will grow, political alliances will fray, and inter-oligarchical conflicts will resume. The failure by the EU to provide enough financial relief to Ukraine will undermine pro-Western feelings in the country. As a result, Ukrainian authorities will lose support inside the country, and Kyiv will have to turn to Moscow for assistance, which it may provide, but on its own terms. (Trenin in Razumkov Centre, 2014: 52)

However, the Russian leadership appeared oblivious to the fact that resorting to military force against its neighbour would severely undermine its political objectives. Russia's attempt to compel Ukraine to federalize – using the separatist republics as instruments to curtail Ukraine's statehood – ultimately failed. In an act of self-preservation, Kyiv chose to accept the de facto loss of control over part of the Donbas rather than compromise its national independence; akin to an animal gnawing off a limb to escape a trap.

Even as late as 2021, Moscow continued to mask its true intentions behind a veneer of international legality: while nominally respectful of Ukraine's statehood, Russia's use of proxies enabled it to present itself as a neutral mediator to an allegedly internal conflict. This duplicitous posture allowed Russia to maintain 'plausible deniability' (Allison, 2014), a narrative accepted by those willing to overlook the underlying manipulation. Upon coming to power in 2019, President Zelensky dashed any remaining hope that Ukraine would accept Moscow's interpretations of the Minsk agreements, which de facto would have embedded Russia's enclaves within Ukraine's domestic political system on Russian terms. In retrospect, Ukraine's rejection of Russia's ultimatums in 2019–20 can be seen as the final straw: the Kremlin ran out of both strategic patience and effective tools.

Patrimonialism unmasked

In 2022, following a century of formal recognition of Ukraine as a sovereign entity and a 'brotherly nation', enshrined in constitutional and, then, international law, Russia rescinded what ultimately proved to be a temporary concession of sovereignty. Much like the annexation of the Baltic states in 1940, 'this was one of the moments in modern Russian history when the mask suddenly drops, all pretences of normality are set aside and the regime's true intentions are laid unmistakably bare' (Moody, 2025: 180).

Following this retraction of recognition, Russia – much like during the Soviet era – mobilized a wide array of arguments, principles and narratives to justify its actions (Kennan, 1961; Darczewska, 2024; Götz and Ekman, 2024; Allison, 2024). One prominent line of reasoning centred on the alleged lack of representativeness of the Ukrainian government. For instance, Foreign Minister Sergey Lavrov asserted, 'I don't think anyone can claim that the Ukrainian regime, since the 2014 coup d'état, represents all the people living on the territory of the Ukrainian state'.[2]

Another set of justifications framed Ukraine's political system as a Western-engineered project designed to perpetuate hostility toward Russia. According to this narrative: 'The Western authors of the anti-Russia project set up the Ukrainian political system in such a way that presidents, members of parliament and ministers would change but the attitude of separation from and enmity with Russia would remain.'[3]

From Moscow's perspective, any international support for Ukraine's sovereignty is interpreted as part of a broader strategy to weaken and fragment Russia. As President Putin declared, such efforts are intended 'to divide our state and set our peoples against each other'.[4]

This aligns with the overarching narrative that frames Ukraine as a historical possession of Russia, wherein any resistance to Russia's efforts to reclaim Ukraine is construed as inherently anti-Russian. In this vein, Putin asserted, '[F]or we are one people', referring to the large Russian nation, a tri-unity comprising Velikorussians, Malorussians and Belorussians; he invoked the 'spiritual, human and civilizational ties formed over centuries' with 'origins in the same sources'.[5] Notably, Putin claimed that Ukrainians inhabit Russian 'historical lands', a framing that implies Ukrainians are accidental occupants – akin to squatters – on territory that rightfully belongs to Russia (Kuzio, 2020).[6]

2 'Russia's Lavrov questions Ukraine's right to sovereignty', Reuters, 22 February 2022, www.reuters.com/world/europe/russias-lavrov-questions-ukraines-right-sovereignty-ifax-2022-02-22.

3 'On the historical unity of Russians and Ukrainians', 12 July 2021.

4 Speech, 30 September 2022, http://en.kremlin.ru/events/president/news/69465.

5 'On the historical unity of Russians and Ukrainians', 12 July 2021.

6 Putin places much of the blame for this on the 'historic, strategic mistakes' of the Bolshevik leaders: 'The collapse of the historical Russia known as

As Darczewska (2024) notes, these narratives are not only complex but also internally inconsistent and contradictory. Nevertheless, their core tenets reflect the foundational logic of Russian patrimonialism: the belief that Ukraine is an integral part of historical Russia and that Ukrainians have no legitimate right to exist as a distinct people unless subsumed within the Russian nation (Chapter 2). The myth of a 'one Russian nation' serves to delegitimize Ukraine's status as a separate (and 'brotherly') nation (Getka, 2024). The invasion thus aims to reverse the historical clock to a pre-Bolshevik era, representing a deliberate return to the 19th-century imperial denial of Ukrainian identity. This perspective was exemplified by the tsarist journalist and editor Mikhail Katkov, who wrote in 1863: 'Ukraine has never had its own history, it has never been an independent state, Ukrainian people are authentic Russian people, indigenous [*korennoi*] Russian people, essential part of Russian people, without which it can hardly remain what it is today' (cited in Plokhy, 2017: 17).

In this sense, Russia's aggression against Ukraine is not solely aimed at reclaiming 'historical lands', but also the people who inhabit them, reintegrating them into the imagined unity of the 'Russian nation' (Darczewska, 2024). Through its invasions in 2014 and 2022, Russia sought not only territorial control but also institutional dominance, thereby enabling it to shape prevailing narratives and identities within the occupied regions (Lewis, 2025; Barbieri, 2025). As Finkel argues, Russia's overarching intent is 'destroying Ukraine as a state, as an identity, and as an idea' (2024: 3). This ambition was echoed by former EU Commission president, José Manuel Barroso, who testified:

> Putin does not want to come to the Russian people and say, okay, we have gained some more territory, a little bit

the USSR is on their conscience', Address, 21 February 2022, http://en.kremlin.ru/events/president/news/67828.

> of Donbass, a little bit of Crimea now. The goal of Putin was to avoid Ukraine to be a country. I know because I spoke with him about this.[7]

Under this logic of patrimonial reclamation, the only acceptable status for Ukrainians is as a regional branch of the Russian people, permitted to exist only within a Russia-controlled political entity. Ukraine's refusal to accept this formula triggered the limited invasion of 2014 and the full-scale invasion of 2022. These invasions represent punitive measures against a 'rebellious province' that needed to be coerced into submission. Similarly, those who refuse to consider themselves Russian are portrayed as enemies, or 'Nazis', who need to be 'neutralized', a rhetoric justifying the violent Russification and ethnic cleansing, including the forcible transfer of children, in the occupied territories (Finkel, 2024; Lewis, 2025).

Moscow asserts that the 'true sovereignty of Ukraine is possible only in partnership with Russia'.[8] In this view, Russia positions itself as the ultimate arbiter of what constitutes a legitimate government in Ukraine. More broadly, it reflects a long-standing prerogative claimed by Russian rulers: the authority to determine whether nations, such as Ukraine, should exist, within what boundaries, and under which form of governance. This marks an explicit return to tsarist-era narratives and practices, completing a full circle in Russia's patrimonial trajectory.

The articulation of these long-suppressed narratives has rendered the acts of recognition of Ukraine in 1922 and,

---

7 '"Putin told me he did not want Ukraine to exist" – Former EU Commission chief, José Manuel Barroso', *Euronews*, 21 November 2024, www.euronews.com/my-europe/2024/11/21/putin-told-me-he-did-not-want-ukraine-to-exist-former-eu-commission-chief-jose-manuel-barr.

8 'On the historical unity of Russians and Ukrainians', 12 July 2021.

more significantly, in 1991, effectively defunct. Ukraine has thus been transformed from a sovereign interlocutor into a subject to be negotiated over, rather than with. While Moscow professes openness to 'negotiations', these are limited in terms of the parameters and nuances of Ukraine's existence – subject to the condition that Russia remains the ultimate arbiter of what form of Ukraine is permissible. Russia's demands in 2025 reflect this logic, calling for the de facto vassalization of Ukraine: involving acceptance of subjugation to Russian authority, relinquishment of territories occupied since 2022, and the acceptance of the remainder of Ukraine to become a Moscow-controlled protectorate. This model explicitly mirrors the Belarusian formula of full political, economic and military domination by Russia, while maintaining the superficial trappings of sovereignty.

The tactics employed to realize Russia's patrimonial ambitions vary in response to the shifting military and diplomatic contexts. While their outcomes remain uncertain, analysing Russia's methods offers valuable insight. The Kremlin's approach to Ukraine is not particularly original but rather an amalgamation of its historically tested strategies for expanding and reclaiming patrimony across Europe. Notably, parallels can be drawn between Moscow's peace plan conditions vis-à-vis Ukraine in 2022 and the Bolshevik demands made to newly independent Poland a century earlier. Following the break-up of the tsarist empire, Poland regained independence in 1918. During the 1920 Bolshevik-Polish war, the Bolshevik government tried to recapture Poland, demanding the installation of a compliant Communist regime, the reduction and disarmament of Poland's military, and restrictions on its sovereignty – all under the guise of safeguarding Russia's security, economic and cultural interests (Davies, 2003). These demands closely mirror those made of Ukraine since 2022.

The historical precedent extends further. Russia's proposals for partitioning Ukraine evoke the dismemberment of Poland in the late 18th century, when Catherine the Great invited

Prussia and the Habsburg Empire to divide the territory of the First Polish Republic (Butterwick-Pawlikowski, 2020). In a striking historical twist, Russia now encourages Poland, Romania and Hungary to claim their own 'historic slice' of Ukraine. This strategy aims to normalize Russia's conquest by presenting territorial division as a conventional European practice.[9]

The craft of legal manipulation

This book sheds light on the extent to which international law has been deployed by Russia in its dealings with Ukraine and Eastern Europe, a dimension of Russian statecraft that has consistently been overlooked or misunderstood. Law – whether domestic or international – is frequently either dismissed as peripheral to the exercise of power, or, conversely, accepted at face value, with the achievement of its professed aims and regulating role assumed to follow. Many observers appear content – or even reassured – by the mere fact that legal procedures have been followed, without critically examining the instrumentalist approach underlying Russia's engagement with the law-making process or the substantive content of the resulting legal norms. As a result, legal façades are maintained until violations become too overt or severe to ignore. When this happens, however, new agreements or settlements with Russia are proposed to replace the ones that Russia violated.

In parallel, scholars ponder over the nature of Russia's actions, with debates frequently confined to a revisionist dilemma. In this case, scholars and experts painstakingly deliberate whether

[9] It is evident that Poland has no intention of claiming any part of contemporary Ukraine or participating in its partition, thereby re-enacting the partitions of Poland orchestrated by Russia at the end of the 18th century. However, in Hungary, the Orban government echoed Russia's narrative by defining Ukraine as a mere 'territory'.

Russia's actions constitute a transformation of existing norms or principles, or whether they represent a form of neo-revisionism or selective revisionism, where violations are contextualized as reactive measures to external pressures (Sakwa, 2019; Götz and Merlen, 2019; Allison, 2020).

In line with this logic, Russia was widely seen as a 'good citizen' of the international system, generally playing by its rules up until 2022 (or at least 2014). This perception underscores the effectiveness of Moscow's use of justificatory smokescreens (Allison, 2014). Indeed, Moscow has deployed various forms of 'lawfare', including portraying itself as the watchdog of international law, ostensibly defending it against the duplicity of the West (Bachmann and Mosquera, 2015; Voyger, 2018). Consequently, distinguishing between rule-breaking and rule-protecting became increasingly difficult – a situation that, while troubling, was hardly surprising, given Russia's strategic intent.

Russia has deliberately cloaked its claims and demands vis-à-vis Ukraine in a range of discourses, including appeals to minority rights and assertions of 'security concerns', thereby constructing a complex, fragmented web of rationalization and justification. This multifaceted narrative poses a significant challenge for contemporary academia, which remains characterized by disciplinary silos that are often discrete, narrowly focused and competing. Such fragmentation hampers the development of a holistic and nuanced understanding of Russia's strategic objectives and the methods by which they are pursued (Stent, 2014).

In particular, the decline in expertise on the tsarist and Soviet legal systems has made it difficult to fully appreciate the enduring continuities in Russia's aims and methods since 1991. We argue that Russia's use of domestic and international law has been central to the exertion of its patrimonial power vis-à-vis Ukraine in the post-Soviet era. Analysing Russia's actions through the conventional paradigms of 'compliance versus violation' or 'revisionism' is insufficient; instead, a shift toward an 'instrumentality' framework is required. This is because Russia has demonstrated considerable skill in deploying international law to serve its needs: it was an important device for signalling 'normality' and thereby obscuring its quest for domination.

Since 1991, law has functioned as a potent instrument in Moscow's patrimonial toolbox, particularly following its depletion after the collapse of the Communist political and economic system, which had previously secured its hold over numerous Central and Eastern European nations. Russia's legal manipulation tactics in the post-Soviet period, which we explored in detail in Chapters 4 to 6, can be best summarized by distinguishing, first, the process of treaty-making and, second, the substance of the agreements resulting from it.

Process

In terms of process, Russia leveraged the significant asymmetry in its power relative to Ukraine. The negotiations on issues from borders to reintegration reveal Moscow's consistent reliance on political and economic pressure, exploiting Ukraine's acute economic dependence and the political vulnerabilities of its elites. Ukraine's domestic weaknesses proved uniquely useful to striking ad hoc, secretive and opaque deals at the highest political level.

Central to this template was Moscow's exploitation of Ukraine's urgent need for legal recognition of its sovereignty, a need that made Kyiv both eager to engage and willing to compromise. Aware of this advantage, Russia's favoured approach was to link the negotiations across disparate policy areas, such as trade, energy and borders, to regional integration, thereby amplifying its leverage. As Moscow became more adept at applying combined pressure, this approach was increasingly deployed, particularly following Vladimir Putin's rise to power in 2000.

Each stage of the treaty-making process – negotiation, initialling, signature and ratification – was treated as an opportunity to exert pressure. By portraying the process as 'work in progress', Moscow effectively employed a 'salami slicing' technique to extract incremental concessions from Ukraine. Simultaneously, it garnered international credit for engaging in bilateral resolution of concerns by treaty-making and ostensibly respecting Ukraine's sovereignty.

Across all areas examined in detail in this book, Russia's approach was deliberately piecemeal. Moscow eschewed agreements which would deal with the issue at stake, such as borders for example, in a comprehensive, detailed and definitive manner. Instead, incremental treaty-making ensured that critical matters remained unresolved, leaving Ukraine in a state of persistent uncertainty. This allowed Russia to retain, and where possible enhance its leverage by conditioning further legal steps on new concessions. Thus, while signalling goodwill to international audiences, bilateral agreements left Ukraine's legal and political position ambiguous and exposed. The fanfare over landmark treaties, such as the 1997 Treaty on Friendship, was followed by protracted negotiations over unresolved issues, leaving Ukraine with a symbolic agreement but a multitude of unfinished business. Russia used this ambiguity to make further demands, as exemplified by the 2003 State Border Agreement, where vital details were postponed, only then to be undermined in subsequent agreements on borders (see Chapter 6).

Substance

In terms of substance, we argue that Russia's agreements with Ukraine bear strong resemblance to Soviet legality, particularly in their extensive use of general, vague and ambiguous legal formulations (Sharlet, 1977). Such ambiguity enabled Moscow to interpret legal norms in a self-serving manner, maximizing its own freedom of action while minimizing its obligations. Simultaneously, this vagueness allowed Russia to portray Ukraine's legal undertakings as far-reaching and binding and undermine Kyiv's efforts to introduce caveats through nuanced drafting.

A key technique in Russia's bilateral agreements was the deliberate limitation of references to international law. This approach was especially evident in the drafting of energy agreements and, for example, the 2003 Azov Sea and Kerch Strait Agreement, where dispute resolution mechanisms were confined to bilateral diplomatic channels. By excluding international legal remedies, these agreements reinforced Russia's negotiating advantage and curtailed Ukraine's ability to seek external adjudication.

The net result was that Ukraine was almost entirely reliant on Russia's legal guarantees, with little more than hope that Moscow would adhere to its rhetorical commitment to legality and that the international system would intervene when necessary. Over time, Ukraine grew increasingly aware of Russia's legal manipulation tactics and more adept in its efforts to limit Russia's leverage. The events of 2014 – when, among others, Russia unilaterally determined which of its agreements with Ukraine remained valid – should have served as a wake-up call for the West too. Russia's 2022 declaration that Ukraine has no right to exist ought to have dispelled any remaining illusions about Moscow's intentions or the restraining power of legal agreements involving Ukraine.

The demand for Western acquiescence and the future of international law

The Kremlin's assertion that the West has compelled Russia to resort to military means in Ukraine in defence of its national interest, reflects a conception of sovereignty as a privilege reserved for a select group of states. This claim reflects the belief that, first, Ukraine lacks the legitimate right to determine its own identity and foreign policy, and, second, that its actions are merely the result of manipulation by external powers, namely the West, which is portrayed as deliberately obstructing Ukraine's 'natural' unity with Russia.

Consistent with Russia's patrimonial logic, international relations are not viewed as 'normal' interactions, governed by agreements in pursuit of their stated goals. Instead, Moscow has interpreted Ukraine's engagement with the EU or the US as an attempt by these actors to establish their own patrimony by turning Kyiv against Moscow. Consequently, any form of agreement with, or support for, Ukraine by Western powers is perceived as a direct threat to Russia's interests.

Russia's efforts to curtail the role of the West were on full display during the period from 1991 to 2014. Russia pursued its objectives toward Ukraine primarily through bilateral relations, while simultaneously presenting itself to the West as the interlocutor and gate-keeper to the post-Soviet space (Dragneva and Wolczuk, 2015b). However, by 2014 it became clear that these bilateral efforts had failed to secure Russia's hold over Ukraine. In response, Russia turned its own failure to coerce Ukraine into friendship into a *problem for* and *of* the West. Paradoxically, while the West is depicted as a competitor and foe (Giles, 2022), it is also increasingly regarded in Moscow as part of the solution. Within this framing, Ukraine is the theatre of a larger conflict between Russia and the West, with the US positioned as a potential enforcer capable of compelling Ukraine into submission. It is in this context that the second Trump administration is viewed not only as a competitor, but also an ally, one that can secure the return of the delinquent Ukraine back to its 'historic master'.

To this end, Russia presents itself as one of the principal global powers in a multipolar world – but strictly on its own terms (Kubica, 2024). At the core of this positioning lies Russia's own view of sovereignty – rooted in patrimonial entitlement – which Moscow wants recognized and accepted by other sovereign states within a reconfigured 'concert of powers'. From Moscow's perspective, sovereignty is not a universal attribute of statehood: only few states are sovereign the rest are just colonies of those great powers.[10] This interpretation of sovereignty legitimizes, in Russia's view, the violation of even peremptory norms of international law, with its war of aggression against Ukraine exemplifying this logic (Allison, 2024). The Russian notion of sovereignty thus includes the prerogative to use force on territories it chooses to define as part of its 'historical lands'. Crucially, this approach is not unprecedented; it reflects a return to 19th- and 20th-century models of territorial expansion and control of conquered territories.

This war, therefore, carries profound implications for the existing international law and order. As Putin declared: 'Russia is a great thousand-year-old power, a whole civilization, and it is not going to live by such makeshift, false rules.'[11] This statement encapsulates Moscow's rejection of the fundamental norms of international law in favor of pseudo-historical narratives (Snyder, 2025). Pseudo-historical myths rather than international law in general, or any agreements in particular, are used to define 'what Russia is' and 'where Russia ends'. This perspective aligns with Russia's endorsement of the view that true sovereignty entails the capacity to claim exceptions to established norms (Lewis, 2020). Such a stance not only undermines the liberal foundations of the rules-based international order but seeks to transform its core tenets (Cavandoli and Wilson, 2022; Allison, 2024). Therefore, in Russia's pursuit of a multipolar world, this transformation 'is no longer limited to repurposing rules and institutions, but extends to redefining the most foundational of legal and political concepts' (Jorgensen, 2022).

This battle for the 'soul' of international law raises two specific and pressing questions. The first concerns the role of

[10] E.g. 'No middle way between being independent country and colony, Putin says', *TASS*, 9 June 2022, https://tass.com/politics/1462989.

[11] Address, 30 September 2022.

negotiations and legal accords as means to pause or end the war. For some, international law remains a relevant framework, or at least a normative benchmark, for crafting a resolution (Weller, 2022; Green et al, 2022). However, many such proposals are drafted in a historical vacuum, as if Russia's record were a clean slate. As Allison aptly asks, 'How can an eventual political and diplomatic settlement of the Russia–Ukraine war be achieved in treaty language and sustained, if trust in Russia's commitment to agreements and its acceptance of Ukrainian statehood has collapsed?' (2024: 281).

Given Russia's long-standing tradition of instrumentalizing legal façades to manage and expand its patrimonial possession, it is evident that legal agreements alone cannot deliver a sustainable solution. While a ceasefire or peace agreement is often viewed as a necessary precondition for ending the war, it is certainly not a sufficient one. To break the pernicious pattern of Russia's policy toward Ukraine, the most basic requirement is robust deterrence and credible Western security guarantees to underpin any negotiations and legal documents signed between Ukraine and Russia (Allison, 2024; Bond, 2025). Unlike in 2014, by 2025 this reality appears to be increasingly understood in Europe, even if such guarantees remain elusive.

The second question relates to the broader implications for neighbouring states beyond Ukraine and for the European security system as a whole. The attack on Ukraine is symptomatic of a far-reaching challenge. As Kennan observed: '[T]he jealous and intolerant eye of the Kremlin can distinguish, in the end, only vassals and enemies, and the neighbours of Russia, if they do not wish to be one, must reconcile themselves to being the other' (2014: 214). For centuries, Russia has employed a range of political and legal instruments to expand and defend its patrimony and carve out a zone in Europe beyond the reach of other 'sovereign states' and international law. Thus, it is clear that this war is not solely about Ukraine – it is also about the future of Europe. Russia's demand for a 'new security architecture' reflects its aspiration to revive a 'concert of powers' model, wherein the United States and Russia negotiate over the fate of Europe.

Conclusions

In this book, we argue that the pre-modern origins of Russian patrimonialism underpin Moscow's proprietary claims over Kyiv and its demands for loyalty from subjugated populations. The concept of patrimony encapsulates a deeply entrenched and all-pervasive fusion of power and ownership. The patrimonial mindset and goals extend far beyond the notion of a mere 'sphere of influence', dynamics that the prevailing Western-centric concepts in law and international relations struggle to grasp.

At the same time, these pre-modern foundations are crucial for understanding not only Moscow's proprietary conception of sovereignty but also its pursuit of international recognition for this paradigm. Russia's approach reflects an effort to reconfigure the international order in line with pre-20th-century norms – specifically, a concert of great powers endowed with exclusive rights. Within this framework, such powers are viewed as the sole legitimate holders of full sovereignty, entitled to alter borders through force, making and unmaking states and nations in the process.

Thus, there should be little doubt about Russia's rationale in invading Ukraine. The war was neither provoked by NATO's enlargement nor the symptom of Putin's singular obsession. Rather, it reflects an enduring domestic imperative to control and expand. It is about a patrimonial model of power: not only a domestic system but also how it extends into foreign policy, shaping relations with neighbouring states (Domanska, 2017). As Pipes reminds us:

> [T]he tenacity with which Russian governments, whatever their professed ideology, have held on to every square inch of land that has ever belong to any of

> them is embedded in the patrimonial mentality. It is a territorial expression of the same principle by virtue of which Russia's rulers have refused voluntarily to concede to their subject one iota of political power. (1994: 79)

Therefore, the attack on Ukraine forms part of a long-term, strategic trajectory of Russia's foreign policy, rooted in the enduring characteristics of its political regime and the deeply ingrained mentality of its ruling elites. Since 1991, Russia has viewed Ukraine's independence as a temporary anomaly: one that must be corrected through voluntary reintegration or, failing that, by force. The so-called 'special military operation' represents an attempt to subdue what is perceived as an insubordinate province, to punish it, and to reassert Russian control. Moscow's demands amount to a diktat: Ukraine must accept a vassal status and restore the political, economic, cultural, linguistic and religious levers of Russian influence.

Against this backdrop, the belief that the 1991 dissolution of the USSR marked the end of Russia's patrimonial hold was both naive and historically uninformed. Nevertheless, this ahistorical view of a 'new Russia' dominated policy thinking in Washington and many Western European capitals for nearly three decades. As argued here, instrumentalizing law – domestic and international – has been a central element of Russia's strategy to reclaim Ukraine. The breadth of tactics employed between 1991 and 2021, ranging from agreements on military bases and energy supplies to regional integration and support for pro-Russian politicians in Ukraine, presents a complex and often overwhelming picture for researchers. It is unsurprising that arriving at a systematic view of Russia's long-term coordinated strategy and legal statecraft toward Ukraine has been a significant challenge.

This book fills this gap. It moves beyond the ad hoc explanations for Russia's aggression, explanations that often take Russia's historical claims, perceived threats and 'security concerns' at face value. Looking forward, the book underscores that legal agreements, while often viewed in the West as instruments of resolution and stability, are not panaceas. Rather, they are integral components of Russia's patrimonial toolbox. Understanding Russia's manipulation of international law is therefore essential to safeguarding against the recurrence of this pernicious pattern.

Bibliography

Allan, D. (2020) 'The Minsk Conundrum: Western Policy and Russia's War in Eastern Ukraine', Chatham House Research Paper, www.chathamhouse.org/sites/default/files/2020-05-22-minsk-conundrum-allan.pdf.

Allison, R. (2012) *Russia, the West, and Military Intervention*, Oxford University Press.

Allison, R. (2014) 'Russian "deniable" intervention in Ukraine: how and why Russia broke the rules', *International Affairs*, 90(6): 1255–1297.

Allison, R. (2020) 'Russian revisionism, legal discourse and the "rules-based" international order', *Europe-Asia Studies*, 72(6): 976–995.

Allison, R. (2024) 'Russia's case for war against Ukraine: legal claims, political rhetoric, and instrumentality in a fracturing international order', *Problems of Post-Communism*, 71(3): 271–282.

Antonov, M. (2012) 'Theoretical issues of sovereignty in Russia and Russian law', *Review of Central and East European Law*, 37: 95–113.

Applebaum, A. (2012) *Iron Curtain: The Crushing of Eastern Europe*, Penguin Books.

Atland, K. (2020) 'Destined for deadlock? Russia, Ukraine, and the unfulfilled Minsk Agreements', *Post-Soviet Affairs*, 36(2): 122–139.

Atland, K. (2021) 'Redrawing borders, reshaping orders: Russia's quest for dominance in the Black Sea region', *European Security*, 30(2): 305–324.

Auer, S. (2015) 'Carl Schmitt in the Kremlin: the Ukraine crisis and the return of geopolitics', *International Affairs*, 91: 5: 953–968.

Bachmann, S.D. and Mosquera, A. (2015) 'Lawfare and hybrid warfare: how Russia is using the law as a weapon', *Amicus Curae*, 102: 25–28.

Bækken, H. (2019) *Law and Power in Russia: Making Sense of Quasi-legal Practices*, Routledge.

Balmaceda, M. (1998) 'Gas, oil and the linkages between domestic and foreign policies: the case of Ukraine', *Europe-Asia Studies*, 50(2): 257–286.

Balmaceda, M. (2013) *Politics of Energy Dependency: Ukraine, Belarus, and Lithuania between Domestic Oligarchs and Russian Pressure*, University of Toronto Press.

Barbieri, J. (2025) 'De-sovereignisation as an instrument of Russia's coercive diplomacy in the context of post-Soviet de facto states: a comparative study of Moldova and Ukraine (2012–2022)', PhD Thesis, University of Birmingham.

Berman, H. (1986) 'Law', in F. Feldbrugge, G. van den Berg and W. Simons (eds) *Encyclopedia of Soviet Law*, Martinus Nijhoff, pp 441–444.

Bettiza, G. and Lewis, D. (2020) 'Authoritarian powers and norm contestation in the liberal international order: theorizing the power politics of ideas and identity', *Journal of Global Security Studies*, 5(4): 559–577.

Bideleux, R. and Jeffries, I. (2007) *A History of Eastern Europe: Crisis and Change*, Routledge.

Bilinsky, Y. (1992) 'Political Relations between Russians and Ukrainians', in P. Potichnyj, M. Raeff, J. Polenski and G. Zekulin (eds) *Ukraine and Russia in their Historical Encounter*, University of Alberta, pp 165–199.

Bond, I. (2025) 'Can Europe save Ukraine – and itself – from Putin and Trump?', Centre for European Reforms, London, September.

Brzezinski, Z. and Sullivan, P. (eds) (1997) *Russia and the Commonwealth of Independent States: Documents, Data, and Analysis*, M.E. Sharpe.

Budjeryn, M. (2023) *Inheriting the Bomb*, Johns Hopkins University Press.

Bukkvoll, T. (2001) 'Off the cuff politics: explaining Russia's lack of a Ukraine strategy', *Europe-Asia Studies*, 53(8): 1141–1157.

Bukkvoll, T. (2004) 'Private interests, public policy: Ukraine and the Common Economic Space Agreement', *Problems of Post-Communism*, 51(5): 11–22.

Busygina, I. and Filippov, M. (2021) 'Trade-offs and inconsistencies of the Russian foreign policy: the case of Eurasia', *Journal of Eurasian Studies*, 12(1): 46–56.

Buszynsky, L. (2003) 'Russia and the Commonwealth of Independent States in 2002: going separate ways', *Asian Survey*, 43(1): 15–24.

Butler, W. (1971) '"Socialist International Law" or "Socialist Principles of International Relations"', *The American Journal of International Law*, 65(5): 796–800.

Butler, W. (2020) *International Law in the Russian Legal System*, Oxford University Press.

Butterwick-Pawlikowski, R. (2020) *The Polish-Lithuanian Commonwealth, 1733–1795*, Yale University Press.

Cassese, A. (2012) 'States: Rise and Decline of the Primary Subjects of the International Community', in B. Fassbender and A. Peters (eds) *The Oxford Handbook of the History of International Law*, Oxford University Press, pp 49–70.

Cavandoli, S. and Wilson, G. (2022) 'Distorting fundamental norms of international law to resurrect the Soviet Union: the international law context of Russia's invasion of Ukraine', *Netherlands International Law Review*, 69: 383–410.

Cooper, J. (2009) 'Russia's Trade Relations with the Commonwealth of Independent States', in E. Wilson-Rowe and S. Torjesen (eds) *The Multilateral Dimension of Russian Foreign Policy*, Routledge.

Cooper, J. (2013) 'The Development of Eurasian Economic Integration', in R. Dragneva and K. Wolczuk (eds) *Eurasian Economic Integration*, Edward Elgar, pp 15–33.

D'Anieri, P. (1999) *Economic Interdependence in Ukrainian-Russian Relations*, State University of New York Press.

D'Anieri, P. (2012) 'Ukrainian foreign policy from independence to inertia', *Communist and Post-Communist Studies*, 45: 447–456.

D'Anieri, P. (2019) *Ukraine and Russia: From Civilized Divorce to Uncivil War*, Cambridge University Press.

Danilenko, G. (1999) 'Implementation of international law in CIS states: theory and practice', *European Journal of International Law*, 10(1): 51–69.

Darczewska, J. (2014) 'The anatomy of Russian information warfare: the Crimean operation, a case study', Centre for Eastern Studies, Warsaw, 42 (May).

Darczewska, J. (2024) *Zawładnąć umysłami i urządzić świat. Rosyjska strategia dywersji i dezinformacji*, Centre for Eastern Studies, Warsaw.

Davies, N. (2003) *White Eagle, Red Star: The Polish-Soviet War 1919–20*, Pimlico.

Dawisha, K. (1997) 'Constructing and Deconstructing Empire', in K. Dawisha and B. Parrot (eds) *The End of Empire?*, M.E. Sharpe, pp 338–360.

Deyermond, R. (2016) 'The uses of sovereignty in twenty-first century Russian foreign policy', *Europe-Asia Studies*, 68(6): 957–984.

Domanska, M. (2017) 'Conflict-Dependent Russia', OSW Study, www.osw.waw.pl/en/publikacje/point-view/2017-11-06/confl ict-dependent-russia.

Domanska, M. (2019) 'Putinism after Putin: the deep structures of Russian authoritarianism', OSW Study, 78.

Domanska, M. (2024) 'Lost in translation: Western misconceptions about Putin's Russia', *Comprehensive Report*, CEPA, https://cepa. org/comprehensive-reports/lost-in-translation-western-misconc eptions-about-putins-russia.

Dragneva, R. (2004) 'Is "soft" beautiful? Another perspective on law, institutions, and integration in the CIS', *Review of Central and East European Law*, 3: 279–324.

Dragneva, R. (2013) 'The Legal and Institutional Dimensions of the Eurasian Customs Union', in R. Dragneva and K. Wolczuk (eds) *Eurasian Economic Integration*, Edward Elgar, pp 34–60.

Dragneva, R. (2018) 'The Eurasian Economic Union: Balancing Sovereignty and Integration', in R. Petrov and P. Van Elsuwege (eds) *Post-Soviet Constitutions and Challenges of Regional Integration*, Routledge, pp 48–70.

Dragneva, R. and de Kort, J. (2007) 'The legal regime for free trade in the Commonwealth of Independent States', *International and Comparative Law Quarterly*, 56: 233–266.

Dragneva, R. and Wolczuk, K. (eds) (2013) *Eurasian Economic Integration*, Edward Elgar.

Dragneva, R. and Wolczuk, K. (2015a) *Ukraine between the EU and Russia: The Integration Challenge*, Palgrave Macmillan.

Dragneva, R. and Wolczuk, K. (2015b) 'European Union Emulation in the Design of Integration', in D. Lande and V. Samokhvalov (eds) *The Eurasian Project and Europe*, Palgrave Macmillan, pp 135–152.

Dragneva, R. and Wolczuk, K. (2016) 'Between dependence and integration: Ukraine's relations with Russia', *Europe-Asia Studies*, 68(4): 678–698.

Duben, B. (2020) ' "There is no Ukraine": fact-checking the Kremlin's version of Ukrainian history', https://blogs.lse.ac.uk/lseih/2020/07/01/there-is-no-ukraine-fact-checking-the-kremlins-version-of-ukrainian-history/.

Dubinin, Y. (2007) 'Historical struggle for the Black Sea Fleet', *Russia in Global Affairs*, 1 (January/March), https://eng.globalaffairs.ru/articles/historical-struggle-for-the-black-sea-fleet/.

Dubinsky, D. and Rutland, P. (2019) 'Russia's legal position in the annexation of Crimea: a critique', *Journal of Soviet and Post-Soviet Politics and Society*, 5(1): 45–79.

Dumoulin, M. (2024) 'Ukraine, Russia, and the Minsk agreements: a post-mortem', ECFR Commentary, https://ecfr.eu/article/ukraine-russia-and-the-minsk-agreements-a-post-mortem/.

Dutkiewicz, J. and Smolenski, J. (2023) 'Epistemic superimposition: the war in Ukraine and the poverty of expertise in international relations theory', *Journal of International Relations and Development*, 26: 619–631.

Eberle, J. (1992) 'Russia and Ukraine: what to do with the Black Sea Fleet?', *The World Today*, 48(8–9): 158–160.

Edinger, H. (2022) 'Offensive ideas: structural realism, classical realism and Putin's war on Ukraine', *International Affairs*, 98(6): 1873–1893.

Felgenhauer, T. (1999) 'Ukraine, Russia, and the Black Sea Accords', WWS Case Study, 2/99.

Finkel, E. (2024) *Intent to Destroy: Russia's Two-Hundred Year Quest to Dominate Ukraine*, Basic Books.

Finnin, R. (2022) *Blood of Others: Stalin's Crimean Atrocity and the Poetics of Solidarity*, Toronto University Press.

Freedman, L. (2014) 'Ukraine and the art of limited war', *Survival*, 56(3): 7–38.

Freedman, L. (2015) 'Ukraine and the art of exhaustion', *Survival*, 57(5): 77–106.

Galeotti, M. (1994) 'The Crimea: Russia's Ukrainian peninsula', IBRU Boundary and Security Bulletin.

Gardner, R. (1964) 'The Soviet Union and the United Nations', *Law and Contemporary Problems*, 29: 845–857.

Geiss, R. (2015) 'Russia's annexation of Crimea: the mills of international law grind slowly but they do grind', *International Legal Studies*, 91: 425–449.

Getka, J. (2024) '"Dekolonizacja I Deimperializacja Potrzebne od Zaraz!" Dekonstrukcja Rosyjskiej Imperialnej Narracji Kulturowej Jako Wyzwanie dla Współczesnej Slawistyki. Białoruś, Polska, Ukraina', *Studia Interkulturowe Europy Środkowo-Wschodniej*, 17.

Giles, K. (2022) *Russia's War on Everybody: And What it Means for You*, Bloomsbury.

Glanville, L. (2013) 'The myth of "traditional" sovereignty', *International Studies Quarterly*, 57(1): 79–90.

Glaz'ev, S. (2011) 'Tamozhennyi soiuz – eto tol'ko pervyi etap integratsii', *Kommersant Ukraina*, 18 April, www.kommersant.ru/doc/1623955.

Götz, E. and Ekman, P. (2024) 'Russia's war against Ukraine: context, causes, and consequences', *Problems of Post-Communism*, 71(3): 193–205.

Götz, E. and Merlen, C.-R. (2019) 'Russia and the question of world order', *European Politics and Society*, 20(2): 133–153.

Grant, T. (2015) 'Annexation of Crimea', *The American Journal of International Law*, 109: 68–95.

Green, J., Henderson, C. and Ruys, T. (2022) 'Russia's attack on Ukraine and the *jus ad bellum*', *Journal on the Use of Force and International Law*, 9(1): 4–30.

Gressel, G. (2021) 'Waves of ambition: Russia's military build-up in Crimea and the Black Sea', ECFR Policy Brief, 21 September, https://ecfr.eu/publication/waves-of-ambition-russias-military-build-up-in-crimea-and-the-black-sea/#the-russian-military-build-up-in-crimea.

Grigas, A. (2015) 'How Russia sees Baltic sovereignty', *The Moscow Times*, 14 July 2015.

Gudev, P. (2018) 'Azovo-Chernomorskii region: novye politico-pravovye realii', *Mirovaia ekonomika I mezhdunarodnye otnoshenia*, 62(10): 91–102.

Hale, H. and Onuch, O. (2022) *The Zelensky Effect*, Hurst Publishers.

Hedenskog, J. (2014) 'Ukraine: Challenges for the Future', in N. Granholm, J. Malminen and G. Persson (eds) *A Rude Awakening: Ramifications of Russian Aggression towards Ukraine*, FOI, pp 51–56.

Hendl, T., Bulryuk, O., O'Sullivan, M. and Arystanbek, A. (2024) '(En)Countering epistemic imperialism: a critique of "Westsplaining" and coloniality in dominant debates on Russia's invasion of Ukraine', *Contemporary Security Policy*, 45(2): 171–209.

Hendley, K. (2022) 'Legal dualism as a framework for analyzing the role of law under authoritarianism', *Annual Review of Law and Social Science*, 18: 211–226.

Hill, F. and Jewett, P. (1994) 'Back in the USSR', Brookings, www.brookings.edu/wp-content/uploads/2016/06/Back-in-the-USSR-1994.pdf.

Hill, F. and Stent, A. (2022) 'Putin's war in Ukraine', Brookings, www.brookings.edu/articles/putins-war-in-ukraine-a-conversation-with-fiona-hill-and-angela-stent/.

Hofmeister, U. (2016) 'Civilization and Russification in tsarist Central Asia, 1860–1917', *Journal of World History*, 27(3): 411–442.

Hrytsak, Y. (2023) *A Brief History of Ukraine: the Forging of a Nation*, Public Affairs.

Hunchak, T. (1977) *The Ukraine, 1917–1921: A Study in Revolution*, Harvard University Press.

Hurak, I. and D'Anieri, P. (2022) 'The evolution of Russian political tactics in Ukraine', *Problems of Post-Communism*, 69(2): 121–132.

Ikenberry, J.G. (2018) 'The end of liberal international order?', *International Affairs*, 94(1): 7–23.

Isaeva, A. (2019) 'Cold War and Its Impact on Soviet Legal Doctrine', in M. Craven, S. Pahuja and G. Simpson (eds) *International Law and the Cold War*, Cambridge University Press, pp 256–270.

Jamestown Foundation (2002) 'Moscow differs with Kyiv's European choice', *Monitor*, 29 April, https://jamestown.org/program/moscow-differs-with-kyivs-european-choice-2/.

Jones, R. (1990) *The Soviet Concept of 'Limited Sovereignty' from Lenin to Gorbachev*, Macmillan.

Jonson, L. (2004) *Vladimir Putin and Central Asia*, Taurus.

Jorgensen, M. (2022) 'The weaponisation of international law in Ukraine', *Volkerrechtsblog*, 15 March, https://voelkerrechtsblog.org/the-weaponisation-of-international-law-in-ukraine/.

Jupille, J. and Jolliff, B. (2011) 'Regionalism in the World Polity', paper for EUSA, Boston, https://aei.pitt.edu/52869/1/JUPILLE.pdf.

Kaczmarska, K. (2015) 'Russia's *droit de regard*: pluralist norms and the sphere of influence', *Global Discourse*, 5(3): 434–448.

Kardas, S. and Konończuk, W. (2015) 'Minsk 2 – a fragile truce', *OSW Analyses*, www.osw.waw.pl/en/publikacje/analyses/2015-02-12/minsk-2-a-fragile-truce.

Kassymbekova, B. (2022) 'On decentering Soviet Studies and launching new conversations', *Ab Imperio*, 2022(1): 115–120.

Kassymbekova, B. and Marat, E. (2022) 'Time to question Russia's imperial innocence', PONARS Eurasia Policy Memo No. 771, www.ponarseurasia.org/time-to-question-russias-imperial-innocence/.

Keenan, E. (1992) Muscovite Perceptions of Other East Slavs before 1654: An Agenda for Historians', in P. Potichnyj, M. Raeff, J. Pelenski and G. Zekulin (eds) *Ukraine and Russia in their Historical Encounter*, University of Alberta, pp 20–38.

Kembayev, Z. (2009) *Legal Aspects of Regional Integration Processes in the Post-Soviet Area*, Springer.

Kennan, G. (1961) *Russia and the West under Lenin and Stalin*, Hutchinson of London.

Kennan, G. (2014) *The Kennan Diaries*, W.W. Norton & Company.

Khodarkovsky, M. (2018) 'Between Europe and Asia: Russia's state colonialism in comparative perspective, 1550s–1900s', *Canadian-American Slavic Studies*, 52: 1–29.

Kleinschmidt, H. (2016) 'The family of nations as an element of the ideology of colonialism', *Journal of the History of International Law*, 18: 278–316.

Kohut, Z. (1986) 'The development of a Little Russian identity and Ukrainian nation-building', *Harvard Ukrainian Studies*, 10: 559–576.

Kohut, Z. (1988) *Russian Centralism and Ukrainian Autonomy: Imperial Absorption of the Hetmanate 1760s–1830s*, Harvard Ukrainian Research Institute.

Kostanyan, H. and Meister, S. (2016) 'Ukraine, Russia and the EU: Breaking the Deadlock in the Minsk Process', CEPS Working Document, No. 423, June.

Kovalov, S. (1968) 'Sovereignty and the international duties of socialist countries', *Pravda*, 26 September 1968, reprinted in *Chronique de politique étrangère*, 23(1–2), Prague 1948–1968, pp 247–250.

Kowal, P., Mink, G. and Reichardt, I. (eds) (2020) *Three Revolutions: Mobilization and Change in Contemporary Ukraine*, Ibidem Verlag.

Kozyrev, A. (2019) *Firebird: The Elusive Fate of Russian Democracy*, University of Pittsburgh Press.

Kramer, M. (2014) 'Why did Russia give away Crimea sixty years ago?', Wilson Centre CWIHP e-Dossier No. 47, www.wilsoncenter.org/publication/why-did-russia-give-away-crimea-sixty-years-ago.

Kubica, L. (2024) 'Ukraine's Position in Russia's Strategic Thinking: Domestic, Regional and International Order', Hybrid CoE Paper No. 20.

Kupchinski, R. (2003) 'The Finlandization of Ukraine', *RFE/RL Poland, Belarus and Ukraine Report*, 5: 37, Part II, 7 October 2003.

Kuzio, T. (1997) 'Borders, symbolism and nation-state building: Ukraine and Russia', *Geopolitics and International Boundaries*, 2(2): 36–56.

Kuzio, T. (2014) *Ukraine-Crimea-Russia: Triangle of Conflict*, Ibidem Verlag.

Kuzio, T. (2020) 'Western histories of "Russia" and Ukraine', E-International Relations, www.e-ir.info/pdf/88286.

Kuzio, T. (2023) 'Imperial nationalism as the driver behind Russia's invasion of Ukraine', *Nations and Nationalism*, 29: 30–38.

Kuzio, T. and Wilson, A. (1994) *Ukraine: Perestroika to Independence*, Basingstoke: Macmillan Press.

Larrabee, S. (1996) 'Ukraine's place in European and regional security', *Harvard Ukrainian Studies*, 20: 249–270.

Laruelle, M. (2013) 'Conservatism as the Kremlin's new toolkit: an ideology at the lowest cost', *Russian Analytical Digest*, 134: 2–4.

Levitsky, S. and Way, L.A. (2002) 'Elections without democracy: the rise of competitive authoritarianism', *Journal of Democracy*, 13(2): 51–65.

Lewis, D. (2020) *Russia's New Authoritarianism: Putin and the Politics of Order*, Edinburgh University Press.

Lewis, D. (2025) *Occupation: Russian Rule in South-Eastern Ukraine*, Hurst Publishers.

Lewis, S. (2019) 'Russia's continued aggression against Ukraine', *The RUSI Journal*, 164(1): 18–26.

Lieven, A. (2022) 'Russia has been warning about Ukraine for decades: the West should have listened', *Time*, 25 January, https://time.com/6141806/russia-ukraine-threats/.

Liik, K., Metodiev, M. and Popescu, N. (2019) 'Defender of the faith? How Ukraine's Orthodox split threatens Russia', *ECFR Policy Brief*, https://ecfr.eu/publication/defender_of_the_faith_how_ukraines_orthodox_split_threatens_russia.

Linde, F. (2016) 'The civilizational turn in Russian political discourse: from pan-Europeanism to civilizational distinctiveness', *The Russian Review*, 75(4): 604–625.

Lupel, A. and Mälksoo, L. (2019) 'A necessary voice: small states, international law, and the UN Security Council', International Peace Institute, www.ipinst.org/wp-content/uploads/2019/04/1904_A-Necessary-Voice_Final.pdf.

Lutsevych, O. (2016) 'Agents of the Russian world: proxy groups in the contested neighbourhood', Chatham House Research Paper, www.chathamhouse.org/sites/default/files/publications/research/2016-04-14-agents-russian-world-lutsevych.pdf.

Lynch, A. (2016) 'The influence of regime type on Russian foreign policy toward "the West", 1992–2015', *Communist and Post-Communist Studies*, 49(1): 101–111.

Lynch, A. (2021) 'Vladimir Putin: Russia's Neo-Patrimonial Façade Democracy', in K. Larres (ed) *Dictators and Autocrats: How They Obtained Power & How They Kept It*, Taylor & Francis, pp 157–173.

Lynch, D. (2000) *Russian Peacekeeping Strategies in the CIS: The Cases of Moldova, Georgia and Tajikistan*, Macmillan.

Mace, J.E. (1983) *Communism and the Dilemmas of National Liberation: National Communism in Soviet Ukraine, 1918–1933*, Harvard University Press.

Magocsi, P.R. (1996) *A History of Ukraine*, University of Toronto Press.

Makarychev, A. and Yatsyk, A. (2014) 'A new Russian conservatism: domestic roots and repercussions for Europe', Notes Internationals CIDOB, www.cidob.org/sites/default/files/2024-07/NOTES%2093_MAKARYCHEV_ANG1.pdf.

Mälksoo, L. (2012) 'Russia-Europe', in B. Fassbender and A. Peters (eds) *The Oxford Handbook of the History of International Law*, Oxford University Press, pp 764–786.

Mälksoo, L. (2015) *Russian Approaches to International Law*, Oxford University Press.

Mälksoo, L. (2021) 'Post-Soviet Eurasia, uti possidetis and the clash between universal and Russia-led regional understandings of international law', *New York University Journal of International Law and Politics*, 53(3): 787–822.

Mälksoo, M. (2022) 'The postcolonial moment in Russia's war against Ukraine', *Journal of Genocide Research*, 25(3–4): 471–481.

Mamlyuk, B. (2019) 'The Cold War in Soviet International Law', in M. Craven, S. Pahuja and G. Simpson (eds) *International Law and the Cold War*, Cambridge University Press, pp 339–375.

Markovits, I. (2007) 'The death of socialist law?', *Annual Review of Law and Social Science*, 3: 233–253.

Marxen, C. (2016) 'International law in crisis: Russia's struggle for recognition', MPIL Research Paper No. 2016–05, https://papers.ssrn.com/sol3/papers.cfm?abstract_id=2771293#.

Matlock, J. (1995) *Autopsy on an Empire*, Random House.

Mearsheimer, J. (2014) 'Why the Ukraine crisis is the West's fault', *Foreign Affairs*, 93(5): 77–84.

Mearsheimer, J. (2022) 'The causes and consequences of the Ukraine War', CIRSD, www.cirsd.org/en/horizons/horizons-summer-2022-issue-no.21/the-causes-and-consequences-of-the-ukraine-war.

Meister, S. (2015) 'Welcome, escalation: why Minsk 2 is not going to work', *DGAPstandpunkt*, No. 2, February, www.europeansources.info/record/welcome-escalation-why-minsk-2-is-not-going-to-work/.

Menon, R. and Rumer, E. (2015) *Conflict in Ukraine: The Unwinding of the Post-Cold War Order*, MIT Press.

Moiseev, A. (2009) *Suverenitet gosudarsttva v mezhdunarodnom prave*, Vostok Zapad.

Moody, O. (2025) *Baltic: The Future of Europe*, John Murray Press.

Morrison, A. (2021) *The Russian Conquest of Central Asia: A Study in Imperial Expansion, 1814–1914*, Cambridge University Press.

Motyl, A.J. (2015) 'The surrealism of realism: misreading the war in Ukraine', *World Affairs*, 177(5): 75–84.

Mullerson, R. (1993) 'The continuity and succession of states, by reference to former USSR and Yugoslavia', *International and Comparative Law Quarterly*, 42: 473–493.

Musafirova, O. (2023) '"Nado govorit" o vykhode na granitzy Ukrainy ne 1991-go, a 2003 goda', *Novaia Gazeta Evropa*, 10 August, https://novayagazeta.eu/articles/2023/08/10/nado-govorit-o-vykhode-na-granitsy-ukrainy-ne-1991-go-a-2003-goda.

Newman, E. and Zala, R. (2018) 'Rising powers and order contestation: disaggregating the normative from the representational', *Third World Quarterly*, 39(5): 871–888.

Office of Soviet Analysis (OSA) (1991) 'The Soviet Cauldron', declassified typescript intelligence memorandum, April.

Oksamytna, K. (2024) 'Russia's status as a colonial power', E-International Relations, www.e-ir.info/2024/11/01/russias-status-as-a-colonial-power/.

Onuch, O. and Sasse, G. (2016) 'The Maidan in movement: diversity and the cycles of protest', *Europe-Asia Studies*, 68(4): 556–587.

Onyshkiv, Y. (2013) 'James Sherr: Ukraine "is in a dangerous situation"', *Kyiv Post*, 23 December, https://archive.kyivpost.com/article/content/euromaidan/james-sherr-ukraine-is-in-a-dangerous-situation-334161.html.

Oppenheim, L. (1912) *International Law: A Treatise*, Vol. 1, http://diue.unimc.it/e-library/oppenheim_vol1.pdf.

Osakwe, C. (1972) 'Socialist international law revisited', *The American Journal of International Law*, 66(3): 596–600.

Osakwe, C. (1985) 'Sovereignty', in F. Feldbrugge, G. van den Berg and W. Simons (eds) *Encyclopedia of Soviet Law*, Martinus Nijhoff, pp 711–713.

OSCE (2017) *Delimitation and Demarcation of State Boundaries: Challenges and Solutions*, Guidebook, www.osce.org/secretariat/363466.

Osiander, A. (2001) Sovereignty, international relations, and the Westphalian myth', *International Organization*, 55(2): 251–287.

Pelenski, J. (1992) 'The Contest for the Kievan Inheritance', in P. Potichnyj, M. Raeff, J. Pelenski and G. Žekulin (eds) *Ukraine and Russia in their Historical Encounter*, Canadian Institute of Ukrainian Studies Press, University of Alberta, pp 3–19.

Pierzynski, G. and Jonathan, J. (2025) 'Patrimonial imperialism: a taxonomy of the causes of the Russo-Ukrainian war', *Journal for the Theory of Social Behaviour*, 55(3): e70007.

Pipes, R. (1954) *The Formation of the Soviet Union: Communism and Nationalism, 1917–1923*, Harvard University Press.

Pipes, R. (1974) *Russia Under the Old Regime*, Penguin.

Pipes, R. (1980) 'Detante: Moscow's View', in E.P. Hoffmann and F.J. Fleron (eds) *The Conduct of Soviet Foreign Policy*, Aldine Publishing Company.

Pipes, R. (1994) *Russia under the Bolshevik Regime 1919–1924*, Harper Collins.

Plokhy, S. (2000) 'The City of Glory: Sevastopol in Russian historical mythology', *Journal of Contemporary History*, 35(5): 369–383.

Plokhy, S. (2014) *The Last Empire: The Final Days of the Soviet Union*, Oneworld.

Plokhy, S. (2015) *The Gates of Europe: A History of Ukraine*, Penguin Books.

Plokhy, S. (2017) *Lost Kingdom: A History of Russian Nationalism from Ivan the Great to Vladimir Putin*, Penguin Books.

Plokhy, S. (2023) *The Russo-Ukrainian War*, Allen Lane.

Poliakova, L. (2003) 'Nakanune EEP: Kuchma protiv diplomatov', *Ukrainskaya Pravda*, 17 September, www.pravda.com.ua/rus/news/2003/09/17/4374367/.

Polyakov, L. (2015) '"Conservatism" in Russia: political tool or historical choice?', Russie.Nei.Visions No. 90, www.ifri.org/en/papers/conservatism-russia-political-tool-or-historical-choice.

Pomeranz, W. (2018) *Law and the Russian State: Russia's Legal Evolution from Peter the Great to Vladimir Putin*, Bloomsbury.

Popova, M. and Shevel, O. (2023) *Russia and Ukraine: Entangled Histories, Divergent States*, Polity Press.

Prizel, I. (1998) *National Identity and Foreign Policy: Nationalism and Leadership in Poland, Russia and Ukraine*, Cambridge University Press.

Pursiainen, C. and Forsberg, T. (2018) 'The Principle of Territorial Integrity in Russian International Law Doctrine', in S.P. Morris (ed) *Russian Discourses in International Law: Sociological and Philosophical Phenomenon*, Taylor and Francis, pp 220–241.

Rakowska-Harmstone, T. and Gyorgy, A. (1979) *Communism in Eastern Europe*, Indiana University Press.

Razumkov Centre (2014) 'The Russia-Ukraine conflict: current situation, consequences, prospects', *National Security and Defence*, 5–6.

Reshetnikov, A. (2024) *Chasing Greatness*, University of Michigan Press.

Robinson, N. (2017) 'Russian neo-patrimonialism and Putin's "cultural turn"', *Europe-Asia Studies*, 69(2): 348–366.

Roeder, P.G. (1991) 'Soviet federalism and ethnic mobilization', *World Politics*, 43(2): 196–232.

Rostow, N. (1981) 'Law and the use of force by states: The Brezhnev Doctrine', *The Yale Journal of World Public Order*, 7: 209–243.

Rudnytsky, I. (1987) *Essays in Modern Ukrainian History*, Canadian Institute of Ukrainian Studies.

Rumer, E. and Kramer, D. (2009) 'Medvedev's message', *The New York Times*, 20 August, www.nytimes.com/2009/08/21/opinion/21iht-edrumer.html.

Saivetz, C. (2012) 'The ties that bind? Russia's evolving relations with its neighbours', *Communist and Post-Communist Studies*, 45: 401–412.

Sakwa, R. (2019) 'Russian neo-revisionism', *Russian Politics*, 4(1): 1–21.

Saunders, D. (1985) *The Ukrainian Impact on Russian Culture*, CIUS.

Schatz, V. and Koval, D. (2019) 'Russia's annexation of Crimea and the passage of ships through Kerch Strait: a law of the sea perspective', *Ocean Development and International Law*, 50(2–3): 275–297.

Shandra, A. (2019) 'Leaked Kremlin emails show Minsk Protocols designed as path to Ukraine's capitulation', *Euromaidan Press*, October, https://euromaidanpress.com/wp-content/uploads/2019/10/Steinmeier_Minsk_report_full.pdf.

Shapovalov, A. (2012) 'Ukraina potorguetsia za svobodnuiu torgovliu', *Kommersant*, 30 July, www.kommersant.ru/doc/1991449.

Sharlet, R. (1977) 'Stalinism and Soviet Legal Culture', in R. Tucker (ed) *Stalinism: Essays in Historical Interpretation*, W.W. Norton, pp 155–179.

Sharlet, R. (1992) *Soviet Constitutional Crisis: From de-Stalinization to Disintegration*, M.E. Sharpe.

Sherr, J. (1997) 'Russia-Ukraine rapprochement? The Black Sea Fleet Accords', *Survival*, 39(3): 33–50.

Sherr, J. (2002) 'Ukraine and Russia: A Geopolitical Turn?', in A. Lewis (ed) *The EU and Ukraine: Neighbours, Friends, Partners?*, The Federal Trust.

Sherr, J. (2006) 'Ukraine's scissors: between internal weakness and external dependence', Russie.Nei.Visions No. 9, IFRI, www.ifri.org/sites/default/files/migrated_files/documents/atoms/files/sherrenglish.pdf.

Sherr, J. (2010) 'The mortgaging of Ukraine's independence', Chatham House Briefing Paper REP BP 2010/01, www.chathamhouse.org/sites/default/files/public/Research/Russia%20and%20Eurasia/bp0810_sherr.pdf.

Sherr, J. (2013) *Hard Diplomacy and Soft Coercion: Russia's Influence Abroad*, Chatham House.

Sherr, J. (2014) 'Reflections on the new East–West discord', *National Security and Defence*, 5–6: 87–91.

Sherr, J. and Kullamaa, K. (2019) 'The Russian Orthodox Church: faith, power and conquest', Special Report, International Centre for Defence and Security, https://icds.ee/en/the-russian-orthodox-church-faith-power-and-conquest/.

Sherr, J. and Gretskiy, I. (2023) 'Why Russia went to war: a three-dimensional perspective', ICDS, https://icds.ee/en/why-russia-went-to-war-a-three-dimensional-perspective.

Sidorenko, S. (2011) 'Poshla torgovlia', *Kommersant Ukraina*, 1 April.

Silina, T. (2015) 'Miny Minska', *Zerkalo Nedeli*, 13 February.

Skaridov, A. (2014) 'The Sea of Azov and the Kerch Straits', in D. Caron and N. Oral (eds) *Navigating Straits: Challenges of International Law*, Brill, pp 220–237.

Smith, G. (1985) 'Union Republics', in F. Feldbrugge, G. van den Berg and W. Simons (eds) *Encyclopedia of Soviet Law*, Martinus Nijhoff, pp 797–799.

Snyder, T. (2022) 'The war in Ukraine is a colonial war', *The New Yorker*, 28 April, www.newyorker.com/news/essay/the-war-in-ukraine-is-a-colonial-war.

Snyder, T. (2025) 'The myths that made Putin's war', *Financial Times*, 23 September.

Socor, V. (2018a) 'Azov Sea, Kerch Strait: evolution of their purported legal status', *Eurasia Daily Monitor*, 10 December, https://jamestown.org/program/azov-sea-kerch-strait-evolution-of-their-purported-legal-status-part-four/.

Socor, V. (2018b) 'Russia says no to OSCE monitors in the Azov Sea and Kerch Strait', *Eurasia Daily Monitor*, 13 December, https://jamestown.org/program/russia-says-no-to-osce-monitors-in-the-azov-sea-and-kerch-strait/.

Sokyrska, V., Krupenya, I. and Didenko, K. (2021) 'Relations between the RSFSR and Ukrainian SSR in the 1920s: diplomatic and administrative-institutional aspects', *Review of Historical Sciences*, 20(2): 79–101.

Solchanyk, R. (1992) 'Ukraine, the (former) center, Russia, and "Russia"', *Studies in Comparative Communism*, 25(1): 31–45.

Solchanyk, R. (1996) 'Ukraine, Russia, and the CIS', *Harvard Ukrainian Studies*, 20: 19–43.

Steinberg, R. (2013) 'Wanted – Dead or Alive: Realism in International Law', in J. Duniff and M. Pollack (eds) *Interdisciplinary Perspectives on International Law and International Relations*, Cambridge University Press, pp 146–172.

Stent, A. (2014) 'Why America does not understand Putin', *The Washington Post*, 14 March, www.washingtonpost.com/opinions/why-america-doesnt-understand-putin/2014/03/14/81bc1cd6-a9f4-11e3-b61e-8051b8b52d06_story.html.

Subtelny, O. (1981) *Ukraine: A History*, University of Toronto Press.

Sumlenny, S. (2024) 'Russia's hidden colonialism: its origins, forms, and the ways to escape it', European Resilience Initiative Center, https://european-resilience.org/analytics/russias-hidden-colonialism-its-origins-forms-and-ways-escape-it.

Surkov, V. (2020) 'Surkov: mne interesno deistvovat' protiv real'nosti', *Aktual'nye Kommentarii*, 26 February, https://actualcomment.ru/surkov-mne-interesno-deystvovat-protiv-realnosti-2002260855.html.

Sutyagin, I. (2015) 'Russian forces in Ukraine', RUSI Briefing Paper, https://static.rusi.org/201503_bp_russian_forces_in_ukraine.pdf.

Szporluk, R. (1976) *The Influence of East Europe and the Soviet West on the USSR*, Praeger.

Szporluk, R. (2000) *Russia, Ukraine and the Breakup of the Soviet Union*, Hoover Institution Press.

Tarasiuk, B. (1996) 'Ukraine in the world', *Harvard Ukrainian Studies*, 20: 9–15.

Tatarenko, A. (2014) 'The legal status and modern history of Crimean autonomy', Verfassungsblog, 2 April, https://verfassungsblog.de/the-legal-status-and-modern-history-of-crimean-autonomy.

Trenin, D. (2011) *Post-Imperium*, Carnegie Endowment for International Peace.

Trenin, D. (2014) 'The Ukraine crisis and the resumption of great-power rivalry', Carnegie Endowment for International Peace, www.jstor.org/stable/resrep13067.

Tsipko, A. (1991) 'The drama of Russia's choice', *Izvestya*, 1 October, in *Current Digest of the Soviet Press*, XLIII(39): 1.

Tsygankov, A. (2010) *Russia's Foreign Policy: Change and Continuity in National Identity*, Rowman & Littlefield Publishers.

Tzimas, T. (2024) 'The impact of the Minsk Agreements on Ukrainian sovereignty', *Journal of Balkan and Near Eastern Studies*, 26(4): 432–451.

Ustymenko, B. (2024) 'On the necessity to adopt a law of Ukraine on the territorial sea of Ukraine in the Sea of Azov and the Kerch Strait and the north-eastern part of the Black Sea', *Black Sea News*, 19 August, www.blackseanews.net/en/read/221078.

Van Herpen, M.H. (2014) *Putin's Wars: The Rise of Russia's New Imperialism*, Rowman & Littlefield.

Velychenko, S. (1992) *National History as Cultural Process*, Canadian Institute for Ukrainian Studies Press, University of Alberta.

Voice of Russia (2014) 'Federalization of Ukraine is the only way from crisis – Lavrov', 31 March.

Voyger, M. (2018) 'Russian lawfare: Russia's weaponisation of international and domestic law', *Journal on Baltic Security*, 4(2): 35–42.

Walker, E.W. (2003) *Dissolution: Sovereignty and the Breakup of the Soviet Union*, Rowman & Littlefield.

Walt, S. (2022) 'Liberal illusions caused the Ukraine crisis', *Foreign Policy*, 19 January, https://foreignpolicy.com/2022/01/19/ukraine-russia-nato-crisis-liberal-illusions/.

Weller, M. (2022) 'Ukraine settlement options: implications of the use of force for a political settlement', Cambridge Initiative on Peace Settlements, https://cambridgepeace.org/wp-content/uploads/2023/03/Weller-Use-of-Force.pdf.

Williamson, J. (ed) (1993) *Economic Consequences of Soviet Disintegration*, Institute for International Relations.

Wilson, A. (1993) 'The Crimean Tatars: a situation report on the Crimean Tatars', International Alert.

Wilson, A. (2015) *Ukraine Crisis: What it Means for the West*, Yale University Press.

Wilson, A. (2016) 'The Donbas in 2014: explaining civil conflict perhaps, but not civil war', *Europe-Asia Studies*, 68(4): 631–652.

Wolczuk, K. (1997) 'Presidentialism in Ukraine: a mid-term review of the second presidency', *Democratization*, 4(3): 152–171.

Wolczuk, K. (2001) *The Moulding of Ukraine: The Constitutional Politics of State Formation*, Central European University Press.

Wolczuk, K. (2009) 'Ukraine and its Relations with the EU', in S. Fisher (ed) 'Ukraine: Quo Vadis?' Chaillot Paper No. 108, EU Institute for Strategic Studies.

Wolczuk, K. (2016) 'Managing the flows of gas and rules: Ukraine between the EU and Russia', *Eurasian Geography and Economics*, 57(1): 113–137.

Wolczuk, K. (2019) 'The Revolutions and Ukraine's European Integration', in P. Kowal, G. Mink and E. Reichardt (eds) *Three Revolutions: Mobilization and Change in Contemporary Ukraine*, Ibidem-Verlag.

Wolczuk, K. (2021) 'Hegemony without leadership: Russia's strategy in the post-Soviet space', *The Brown Journal of International Affairs*, 28(1): 1–13.

Wolczuk, R. (2002) *Ukraine's Foreign and Security Policy 1991–2000*, Routledge.

Yekelchyk, S. (2007) *Ukraine: Birth of a Modern Nation*, Oxford University Press.

Zaborsky, V. (1995) 'Crimea and the Black Sea Fleet in Russian-Ukrainian relations', Belfer Center for Science and International Affairs, Harvard Kennedy School, Discussion Paper, September, www.belfercenter.org/publication/crimea-and-black-sea-fleet-russian-ukrainian-relations.

Zaslavsky, V. (1992) 'Nationalism and democratic transition in postcommunist societies', *Daedalus*, 121(2): 97–123.

Zhurzhenko, T. (2007) 'Ukraine's border with Russia before and after the Orange Revolution', www.bmlv.gv.at/pdf_pool/publikationen/ukraine_zerissen_zw_ost_u_west_m_malek_ukraines_border_t_zhurzhenko.pdf.

Zhurzhenko, T. (2021) 'A Border on the Move', in H.-K. Peterlini and J. Donlic (eds) 'Beyond Borders', *Yearbook of Migration and Society*, 2020–21, pp 329–354.

Zubok, V. (2021) *Collapse: The Fall of the Soviet Union*, Yale University Press.

Zygar, M. (2023) *War and Punishment: The Story of Russian Oppression and Ukrainian Resistance*, Weidenfeld & Nicolson.

Index

References to tables appear in **bold** type. References to footnotes show both the page number and the note number (72n5).

L

M

N

R

S

V

W

Y

Z

www.ingramcontent.com/pod-product-compliance
Lightning Source LLC
Chambersburg PA
CBHW071928260226
40302CB00062B/21